SO YOU WANT TO BE AN
INSURANCE AGENT

A Step-By-Step Approach to a Successful Insurance Agency

Third Edition

JEFF HASTINGS

ChartHousePress.com

So You Want to Be an Insurance Agent

Third Edition (2013-2015)

By Jeffrey L. Hastings, LUTCF

© 2008, 2009, 2013 by Jeffrey L. Hastings

ISBN: 978-0-9790036-4-6

Chart House Press, LLC.
11200 Westheimer Rd. #520
Houston, TX 77042
281-752-6565

www.ChartHousePress.com

Jeff@JeffHastingsAgency.com
JeffHastingsAgency.com
www.twitter.com/BetterBizCoach
http://www.linkedin.com/in/JeffLHastings
coach.emyth.com/jeffhastings

Edited by: Amy Bell, WritePunch Inc. writepunch.com

Book Design by: Susan Daffron, Logical Expressions, Inc. logicalexpressions.com

Contents

ACKNOWLEDGEMENTS

To say that this book is "by Jeff Hastings" is an overstatement. Without the contributions of a number of people, not only would the creation of this book not have been possible, it is almost certain that my success would have been drastically limited.

Since the first book was printed in 2008, I have received hundreds of emails, phone calls and even a few handwritten notes telling me about what the book meant to my readers. I never expected this type of response and it brings me so much joy to know that I have touched people's lives in a positive way. So first of all, thank you to everyone who has read the book, told someone about it or passed a copy along to a friend. You are truly appreciated.

The first individual that I would like to thank, I have never met and, until a few years ago, had never communicated with. Michael Gerber, the founder of EMyth Worldwide (emyth.com) is the bestselling author of *The E-Myth Revisited, The E-Myth Manager, The E-Myth Contractor,* and *The E-Myth Physician,* as well as a highly sought-after speaker and small business revolutionary. Throughout the years, I have read every book, listened to every tape and watched every video he has produced in an effort to work *on* my business instead of working *in* it. Throughout the writing of my books, it has been difficult for me to remember where his teachings left off and my ideas began. Nonetheless, I feel it extremely necessary to thank the one man who has inspired me to create a business that has truly given me the opportunity to create a better life.

Today, the EMyth organization is reaching new heights under the leadership and direction of C.E.O. Jonathan Raymond. Through the new EMyth cloud-based platform and business coaching process, the company has the ability to reach a much larger audience in all levels of business. I was so excited about the new business strategy; I applied and was accepted to become one of the first contract EMyth Certified Business Coaches under the new leadership in 2012. I am honored to carry on the tradition of helping business owners create a better life — a mission Mr. Gerber started more than 35 years ago.

To get the latest business advice or find events in your area, you can keep up with Jonathan on Twitter (@jonathanraymond) or the EMyth organization at (@emyth).

FOREWORD

Insurance affects everything and everything affects insurance. It is generally understood that insurance protects personal assets and allows those who participate in the economy to produce goods and services without the paralyzing fear that some adverse incident could leave them destitute or unable to function. However, few people are aware of the extraordinary impact the industry has on state, local and national economies far beyond its core function of helping to manage risk.

In his new book, *So You Want to Be an Insurance Agent*, Jeff Hastings gives his readers useful insight into what he believes it takes to become successful in this highly competitive, challenging and potentially high-income career. Twenty-eight years of experience, fifteen of which he has spent recruiting and training agents in the Houston, Texas area, have given him the knowledge to help aspiring agents enter the field successfully.

With the many ongoing changes to insurance contracts across the nation, it is now more important than ever for consumers to have a trusted advisor to help find the right insurance products to fit their needs. Consumers want and need a professional agent to recommend types of coverage and, more importantly, to inform them when there are gaps in their insurance protection. For many people, their home is their greatest asset. Yet, studies show that far too many homeowners in America today are underinsured.

The need for a professional agent became even more apparent after Hurricane Katrina ripped through six southern states in 2005, causing $41 billion in insured losses and flooding tens of thousands of homes, many of which had no flood insurance, leading to devastating results. With catastrophe losses in 2011 exceeding $32 billion, Mother Nature delivered yet another of her increasingly frequent reminders that anything other than full and complete coverage could jeopardize the typical American family's asset.

I encourage those of you who decide to take on the challenge of becoming a professional insurance agent not to take the role lightly. Once you are licensed, try to learn everything you can about the products you are offering and take the time to sit down and explain the coverage options to your customers. Implementing the ideas in Jeff's book can help you create a solid business plan, and, eventually, a successful, thriving agency. Most importantly, as an insurance agent, you can make a significant difference in the lives of the people who have entrusted you to protect their assets.

I wish you the best of luck in your new career!

Dr. Robert P. Hartwig
President
Insurance Information Institute

INTRODUCTION

"If you love what you do, you'll never work a day in your life!" is often said by people who have taken advantage of one of the many small business opportunities that are available in America today. Yet, we all know that while some people grab life by the horns and take control of their own destiny, many others allow their lives to be controlled by others and simply wait for the opportunities that never seem to come. Do you have any friends or family members who always seem to get that lucky break? They always seem to be in the right place at the right time. Why is that? What makes them different?

Happy, successful people have learned to make the most of every day. They are excited about the future and willing to sacrifice today to have a better life tomorrow. This enthusiasm and optimistic attitude allows them to take a chance on their future and take advantage of opportunities as they arise.

Like it or not, your future is in your control! The outcome of your life is a direct result of the decisions you make or fail to make. Many people go through life blaming others or circumstances for their own failures. They sit in thankless jobs complaining about lack of income, lack of respect and a lack of advancement in their careers. Their only hope for a brighter future is to win the lottery. Unfortunately, that never happens. Emotionally and often financially drained, many give up and accept life as they see it—a boring, unfulfilling experience with little reason to try. A few finally decide to take control of their future to seek out the American Dream and open their own business.

What does the American Dream mean to you? In his legendary "I Have a Dream" speech, Dr. Martin Luther King, Jr. described a world of racial equality and the vision of a better life. While you may have your own personal twist on the American Dream, I'm certain that somewhere in your definition is a desire to create a better lifestyle defined in some way by personal wealth.

In a world filled with "get rich quick" schemes, multi-million dollar sports contracts, state lotteries, reality idol contests and asking "who wants to be a millionaire," I believe our society has eroded the dream and replaced it with the belief that shortcuts and luck are the only ways to get ahead. The truth is there are no short cuts in life. There is no substitute for hard work and some sacrifice to achieve financial success.

Most people enter business for themselves after becoming frustrated with their current situation and believing that owning their own business is the answer to their prayers. Corporate downsizing, limited financial opportunities and job instability make the idea of controlling your own future appealing, but before making such a decision, you should first make sure that owning your own business is right for you.

There are unquestionably many Americans who enter this field, work extremely hard, sacrifice personal time and are rewarded significantly for their efforts while others are not so fortunate. Having a dream is common. In fact, as you would expect, 100 percent of the insurance agents I have hired dreamed of success when they began their career. What may surprise you is that I truly believe the ones who failed didn't fail because their dreams were too big, but rather their dreams were too small and, as a result, their approach was too conservative.

It is estimated that 14 percent of the full-time labor force is now self-employed. It is a well-documented fact that 40 percent of them never make it past the first year, and 80 percent of them never make it to the fifth year. What may have been lost in the numbers are the countless business owners who make it, but are unhappy and would have been better off taking a corporate job with a nice retirement plan and corporate benefits. If you weren't paying attention, let me say it again: Eighty percent of small business owners will fail before they see their fifth year!

Business guru Michael Gerber taught us many years ago that the reason so many small businesses fail is most people who go into business have little to no understanding of how to truly make it work. The insurance sales rep opens an insurance agency, the Realtor® opens her own real estate office and the mortgage processor opens his own mortgage company. Most of them have no idea that quoting an insurance policy, selling a home or closing on a mortgage has anything to do with running a business! It is not until they open an office, hire employees and start marketing their services that they realize they are in over their heads and have nowhere to turn.

Now that I have your attention, I can go back to being the optimist that I am. Thank God 20 percent of people who start their own businesses are successful, and I believe I can safely assume they live happy, self-fulfilling and productive lives. What is it that these 20 percent know that the others don't?

Like most people, you probably have little to no idea of how to start your own business. If you do, you probably have had little to no formal training on how to do it right. The good news is that the success rate of new insurance agencies is significantly higher than that of most start-up ventures. The reason for this is simple: In most cases, people are required by either the State Department of Insurance or a mortgage company to purchase the products we sell. Whether or not you ever contact your customers again, every time they renew their policies you are paid a commission until they find a better price or product from one of your competitors.

The fact of the matter is you can earn a significant income and live the American Dream after a few hard years of developing your own agency. However, you must first understand the difficulty in getting this business started and determine if you are ready to take on the challenge.

In the Acknowledgements section of this book, I mentioned the hundreds of emails and phone calls that I've received after writing the First Edition of this book in 2008 and what they have meant to me over the years. Well, not all of the emails I have been entirely positive. In fact, just a few years ago, an insurance executive from a very large insurer sent me an email to tell me how he believed the book was the best he had read about starting a new agency. In fact, he wanted to make it a required reading to all of his company's new hired agents in the future. OK, so that part was positive. But then he went on to state because I had been so negative about how hard it was to start up an agency, he couldn't recommend it and requested that I "re-word" a few chapters. Well, I didn't write the book for him now did I? I wrote the book for you!

The way I figure it, you purchased this book for one of two reasons. Either, 1) you are considering opening an agency and are conducting research or, 2) you have an agency now and are looking for ways to take your agency to a whole new level. OK, maybe 3 reasons...you may be my mother and you felt obligated to buy it when you saw it at Barnes & Noble. Thanks again mom. Regardless of why you purchased it, I have an obligation to you. This could be a life changing decision and the very book you are holding in your hands can give you some clarity to determine if this decision is the correct one. Knowing how important this decision is to you, it is just as important to me that I give you real, honest and useful information to help you along the way. And I'm sorry, but not everything you read is going to be positive and I hope you understand.

After reading this book, you will either be extremely excited and anxious to start your new career, or convinced the risks associated with starting your own business are too great. Listen to your inner self as you read through the chapters. It's this instinct built inside your subconscious that will guide you in the right direction.

In this book, I will give you a step-by-step approach on how to make your dream of owning a successful insurance agency a reality. Regardless of your current level of success or insurance background, you can do it! I know these steps work because they have worked for me and the many people I have helped during more than fifteen years of building my own team of agents while working as a District Manager for the Farmers Insurance Group of Companies. I'm confident that if you decide this is the career for you and you incorporate the lessons I write about in the chapters that follow, you will be happier than ever before, controlling your own destiny and living a life that you may have never thought possible. Let's get started!

PART I

Discovering Your Passion

To every man, regardless of his birth, his shining, golden opportunity…the right to live, to work, to be himself, and to become whatever thing his manhood and his vision can combine to make him.

— Thomas Wolfe

I magine you could be all of who you are when you're at work. Do you know what's stopping you? If you're in a leadership position, understanding what drives you is the single most important factor in the success of your business. It's doesn't matter what drives you. It could be your love of design, your love for food or your passion for helping people get connected. It only matters that you are aware of what drives you. Everything about your business starts here. Getting to know yourself at this level will change the way you manage, and how you think about your brand all the way down to the smallest interactions your staff has with your customers. Who you are is the thread that holds the whole thing together. That is the philosophy of the EMyth and is discussed in detail in their lesson titled *Values, Passion and Purpose (2012)*.

Values, Passion and Purpose© is designed to help you discover the things that matter to you most. There are hundreds if not thousands of business consulting companies out there to choose from. It's the starting point and focus of the EMyth that caught my attention and intrigued me enough to learn more. Please allow me to explain.

As you will find out later in the last chapter in this book, my definition of success was far different just a few years ago than it is today. When I'm asked what success means to me I have narrowed it down to one word — happiness. So in order for my business to be defined in my book as successful, I have to first ask myself if my business adds to my happiness or if it takes it away.

In complete honesty, there are still times when I don't feel all that successful. Working long hours and missing my treasured evening golf cart rides with my three-year old son Logan through the woods sometimes brings me a little down. Hey, don't laugh — I don't play golf and I live in the country. Going 20 mph at night through the woods with big tires and a four-wheel drive golf buggy is a lot more fun than you think! Anyway, over the past few years I've learned to better manage my time so I can live a longer, happier and have a more successful life.

The only way I can own a business that gives me this type of lifestyle is to create a business that truly works. I'm talking about owning a business that is so successful, you can take a month off and your sales don't miss a beat, your customers continue to have the same outstanding service and you know your agency is in good hands because your staff understands their role and is excited to play their part. That is the EMyth perspective and that is why I've partnered up with this incredible organization.

If you were given the opportunity to complete the *Values, Passion and Purpose©* worksheet on emyth.com, you would start by answering these questions:

1. Who are you?

2. Why do you do what you do?

3. What really matters to you in your life?

4. What do you want to share with the world?

From this starting point, you start to determine what your core values are, how you see your life now and more importantly, how you want it to become in the future. We all know we need a business plan and a mission statement for our business, but very few people have ever taken the time to write a plan or vision statement for their life. Just think about what you just read and let it sink in for a moment. Think about what you would say if you wrote a vision statement for your life?

Having a hard time with this? If so, let's try something different. I want you to concentrate for a moment. If you could hear my voice and didn't have to read, I would ask you to close your eyes and imagine you are 10 years older and you are sitting in your doctor's office. Not the clinic, but in her actual business office. She's busy and you are patiently waiting in her guest chair and scanning through art on the wall, accreditations and even glancing at the papers on her desk just to get some idea of what it is she wants to tell you. You know the news couldn't be all that good but are hoping for the best. She walks in and says "hi" but you can tell on her face that something is wrong. Instead of sitting in her chair, she grabs a file from her desk and sits down next to you. Like a good doctor, she doesn't beat around the bush and tells you the results of your medical exams came back and your life expectancy is six months at best, if not just three. She tells you she is very sorry and you can tell by her expression she is sincere. But that doesn't take the horrible feeling you have inside of you with the realization of how your life has suddenly changed.

Now back to present day. If you knew this was going to happen to you 10 years from today, what would you change about your life? Keep in mind; this is 10 years from now. Unless you are financially independent, you are going to have to create income for you and your family. How would you spend your day? Who would you spend it with? How do you want to be remembered?

The fact is that one day we are going to all be faced with death. It could happen in 10 years or in just 10 days. And I believe that if we are fortunate enough to get, as my dad used to say, a "two-minute warning", we would live those last few years, months or even two minutes quite differently. I don't believe when we know our time has come to an end and we reflect back on our lives that it will be the cars we drive, the house we live in or the money we've earned that we will be most proud of. I believe it will be the lives we touched, the places we've seen and the difference we made that will mean the most.

I was teaching an EMyth workshop to a group of insurance agents in late 2012 and we went through the process of writing our own eulogy. I know this sounds morbid and quite honestly, I was a little concerned how this process would turn out. One week later, I had the group of agents back in the meeting room and after our morning session; I asked if anyone had taken the time to complete their business development work from the week before. One of my agents named Michelle raised her hand.

To give you a brief story about Michelle, I have known her for many years. She started out working for one of my agents and I met her in 1998. At that time, her son Vinny was only a young boy and used to come in the office and play after school. The agent she worked for as a customer service representative retired in 2002 and she considered opening her own agency. Nervous about being a single parent, she passed up the opportunity and went to work for another agent. It wasn't until her new boss retired in 2011 when she came to me and said that Vinny was joining the Marines and she was finally ready to control her own destiny. It was a happy day for both of us.

The main point of giving you her background is to tell you she became a close friend. I had been with her through many hard times and the toughest was when her mother passed away in 2006. Michelle is now married and her incredible but very shy husband Mike joined her for our meetings.

During lunch, I asked Michelle if she minded if we read her eulogy aloud to the group. She agreed and just to push it a little further, I asked Mike if he could be the one to read it. Mike looked more nervous than a turkey in November, but reluctantly agreed. Without even seeing or hearing it before, Mike walked up to the podium and started to read.

Words cannot describe the emotion that was felt in that moment. You could truly feel how much Mike loved his wife as he struggled to read each sentence. Pausing at times to hold back the tears, he read the eulogy of his wife like she was no longer with us. Nodding in agreement more than once at Michelle's carefully chosen words, he had to completely stop when he read about what a wife and mother Michelle had become. When Mike finished, there wasn't a dry eye in the room including my own.

If you have never written your own eulogy and really thought about what you wanted to do with your life, I encourage you to do it as soon as possible. Make it fun and get your spouse and teenage/adult children to do the same. Take turns reading each other's eulogy out loud to the family. If a eulogy seems too difficult to do, just write down a Bucket List of things you would like to do before you die and add in a few lines about how you would like to be remembered. I know very few people reading this book will actually do this — but if you do, be careful — something will change!

Having a deep, meaningful and personal conversation with your loved ones like this can mean so much. Word it correctly and old wounds can be healed and love can grow where you thought it had faded. Express yourself and allow those close to you to do the same. It's from this perspective that you may find your motivation to live life differently and bring new meaning to each and every day. It is from this perspective you can visualize the answers to the question asked before, "What do you want to do with your life?"

After you answer this question and then discuss it with your loved ones, you will have a clearer picture of what it is that your business should provide for your life. So this is our starting point: *Values, Passion* and *Purpose*. Define success and begin to live life more intentionally!

PART II

The Basics

*Opportunity is rare, and a wise man will
never let it go by him.*

– Bayard Taylor

What is an insurance agent anyway? For the most part,
insurance marketing is done by agents. An insurance
agent is anyone authorized by an insurer to solicit, create,
modify and terminate insurance contracts. Agents' powers
rest primarily on the authority granted in the agency contract. However, the power to bind the insurer extends beyond the contractual authority granted by the insurer.

Insurance agents have three kinds of authority. First, the
agent has the *stipulated or expressed authority* given by the insurer. The insurer publishes underwriting guidelines identifying eligibility requirements, types of coverage and the
amount of coverage that can be written.

Secondly, the agent has *implied authority*. The law gives agents that power which the public may reasonably believe them to have. In disputed issues, court decisions are based on what is reasonable for the public to believe and the actions that are necessary and customary for agents to perform.

Thirdly, the agent has *apparent authority* which goes beyond expressed and implied authority. If agents lead a buyer to believe they have the power to provide coverage that is not expressed or implied by the insurer, the courts may hold that apparent authority exists.

Why Do People Buy Insurance?

People purchase insurance for a variety of reasons—some logical, some emotional, some because the law requires it. It is helpful to know why people buy before you make a phone call or mail out your first postcard.

Most people buy insurance because they are afraid of experiencing a loss. There are several ways to manage the risk associated with losing something of value: risk avoidance, loss control, retention of risk and transfer of risk.

Risk avoidance is the elimination of the risk in part or in whole. Choosing not to buy a trampoline for your children is a good example. *Loss control* is trying to minimize the likelihood of a loss or the severity of the loss. This might mean purchasing a trampoline with padded bars and a safety net. *Retention of risk* means finding a way to assume the risk personally for the potential of loss. Saving money to pay for the medical bills of an injured child or to pay for a liability claim resulting from a neighbor's lawsuit would be a way of retaining the risk.

Transfer of risk is the preferred method of minimizing risk of financial loss. Generally, this means purchasing insurance.

How Does an Agent Earn Money?

First of all, you cannot earn commissions, recommend coverage or even quote an insurance policy without being properly licensed. In most states, insurance agents are independent contractors and are paid commissions for every policy they sell. In other words, agents are not paid until they are completely licensed *and* close a sale.

Some companies offer up-front money, business lines of credit and/or a subsidized income to help agents get started. In most cases, the companies that offer less up-front incentives and fewer guarantees offer higher commission rates and better long-term potential.

Industry Revenue

According to the Department of Commerce, the insurance industry is one of the largest industries in terms of revenue. The industry accounted for $1.4 trillion in revenues and $121 billion in payroll, according to the agency's latest economic census. These numbers may be a little hard to digest. In my area, the average property and casualty agent with five or more years of service earned $209,376 in annual commissions in 2011 with the top 10 percent earning over

$564,000 per year. This figure can be significantly different in your area.

Types of Agency Ownership

What is a Sole Proprietor?

By definition, a sole proprietorship has only one owner. If you have a business partner, you may be a partnership or choose a different business form, but you cannot operate as a sole proprietorship.

A sole proprietorship is the simplest form of business to start. Ordinarily, all you need to do is start operating as a business under your own name (or a fictitious name), a social security number and any required licenses or permits. There are some distinct disadvantages to operating as a sole proprietorship, which you should consider before deciding if this business form is right for you.

What is a DBA?

In most jurisdictions you may do business under your own name. However, if you wish to use a variation of your name or a completely different business name, you may register a DBA ("doing business as"), so that you may lawfully conduct business under a fictitious name.

Usually, DBAs are filed at the county level, but in some cases they may be filed with the state. You can file your DBA at your local county courthouse. When you register a DBA, the clerk who processes your application will check to make sure that no one else is using the same name you requested.

They will also maintain a record of your real identity for anyone who wishes to find out who is operating under the assumed business name. Certified copies will be given to you at a nominal cost. To open a bank account, you must present a certified copy of your DBA certificate to the bank.

There are some services that will research your business name and file your DBA on-line for a fee. The cost for this service can be as high as $200.

What is a Corporation?

Since you will be in the business of recommending insurance coverage to protect assets, you may want to incorporate at some point. A corporation is a separate legal entity with its own identity separate and apart from its shareholders (owners). As a separate legal entity, a corporation is responsible for its own debts. Normally, shareholders, directors, and officers are not responsible for corporate liabilities. If the corporation suffers losses, its resources are used to cover those losses, not the personal assets of the individual shareholders. Thus, the corporation protects the owner of a business against personal liability.

Other advantages include the following:

- Selling stock to raise capital is often more attractive to investors than other forms of equity.

- A corporation can continue to exist after the death of its founders.

- Stockholders may distribute their interest in the corporation without the corporation dissolving.

- Corporations have many tax options available, including setting-up pension, profit sharing and stock option plans.

If you are planning to sell variable products, mutual funds or investments to your customers, your investment firm may not be able to make checks payable to a corporation. Before spending the money, make sure you get answers to these questions.

How Do I Incorporate?

It is very easy to incorporate. The question of whether or not to incorporate is very complex. Although it is not necessary to have an attorney set up your corporation, I strongly recommend you consulting with a lawyer and a CPA to make certain it is right for you. Most attorneys charge around $500–$1,500 to process the paperwork to form a corporation.

Every state requires you to complete an Articles of Incorporation form and pay a filing fee before approving your application. It's important to note that many insurance companies have specific ways in which your Articles of Incorporation must be filed. Do not process your paperwork until you have approval from your company.

Sole Proprietor or Incorporate?

If you are simply incorporating to save money on taxes, check with your CPA. Recent tax laws have given sole proprietors many of the tax advantages once only afforded to corporations. Most CPAs will tell you that you will pay about the same amount of money to Uncle Sam if you are a sole proprietor or a corporation; however, you will pay the CPA significantly more if you chose to incorporate.

Here are the benefits to incorporating as I see them:

- **Protection against personal liability.** If you chose to be a sole proprietor, make certain you have at least a $1,000,000 personal umbrella policy and a good errors and omissions policy (E&O) in force at all times.

- **Easy to manage tax liability.** When you incorporate, you become an employee of the corporation. You will receive a paycheck in the same manner as the other employees in your business. Taxes will be withheld from your check every time you draw funds from the business. This helps you stay on top of the tax liability because it forces you to pay as wages are earned and to withhold taxes for payment to the government.

- **Better financial records.** A former auditor for the IRS informed me that the IRS targets sole proprietors for audit. Most corporations have very good record keeping processes and CPAs that keep them honest. On the other hand, a larger number of sole proprietors cut corners and have lackluster financial controls. These loose financial controls make it easy for tax auditors to find additional funds due to the IRS. This alone is enough to make most small business owners incorporate!

I highly recommend your consulting with a tax attorney before making the final decision as to what type of business ownership is best for you.

Licensing

In order to become an insurance agent, you must first become licensed. Every state has similar, but unique licensing requirements. Contact your state's Department of Insurance to find out what specific requirements are necessary before you can begin selling. Many states even require extensive pre-licensing requirements.

As a multi-line insurance agent, you will have to pass your Property and Casualty exam, which will enable you to write insurance on automobiles, homes, businesses and personal property. You will also have to pass your Life and Health exams.

Some companies require you to become a registered representative, offering financial services as a part of your product portfolio. A Series 6 and 63 license allows you to offer variable life insurance, variable annuities and mutual funds in your agency. A Series 7 license allows you to offer securities. However, most insurance companies do not require their agents to hold this license.

There are many companies that can help you study for your exams. I have found Test Teachers (testteachers.com), Kaplan Financial and AD Banker & Company (adbanker. com) to be among the best. Kaplan's contact information and each state's specific licensing criteria are listed in Appendix J in the back of this book.

Costs to Get Licensing

The cost for licensing varies by state. Below is an example of some of the costs to obtain a license in Texas:

Property & Casualty exam manual	$49
Drill and practice exams on CD-Rom	$55
Property & Casualty classroom instruction (2 days)	$199
Appointments with your company	Varies
Drill and practice for Life & Health CD-ROM	$55
Life & Health license exam manual	$49
Life & Health classroom instruction (2 days)	$199
Series 6 and 63 exam/registration fees (approximate)	$1000

Bank Accounts, Records and the IRS

I can't tell you how many times I've talked with business owners who had developed multi-million dollar businesses only to be forced to shut down due to their lack of financial control. In our business, there will be ups and downs in your monthly gross income; especially during your early years. The winter months are notoriously slow. Now that you know this, plan for it!

As with any business, you must separate your personal and business expenses. The moment you use a personal credit card or check for a business expense, it can open your entire personal accounts up for audit by the Internal Revenue Service.

If you are not already using financial software to manage your finances, don't delay another day. When you open your business, there will be enough to learn and if you spend too much time trying to figure out how to pay bills and categorize accounts, it will significantly impact your success. I have used QuickBooks® for years and have found it to be an outstanding financial software package for small businesses.

Open your financial accounts in your business name at your local bank. As a new business, it may be beneficial to apply for a line of credit immediately. Even if you don't believe you need it, your business may take a little longer to get started than you may estimate. Your credit score may also take a hit shortly after you leave a "secure job" to become a small business owner. A line of credit may give you the cushion you need during the early years of business with an interest rate you can live with.

Pay off personal debt before paying off business debt. You can write off the interest you pay on your business credit cards, but not on personal ones. In the best case scenario, never carry credit card debt!

Payroll Services

If you fail to pay your income taxes in a timely manner, you will pay significant late penalties. If you fail to pay your employees withheld payroll taxes, your business can be shut down by your state's workforce commission! Don't take a chance and try to process payroll on your own. You need to be focused on building your business.

There are only twenty-four hours in the day, and you cannot afford to be doing $10 per hour work. Research and hire a professional payroll service to process your payroll, complete your 940 and 941 reports, process your W-2s and prepare your 1099s. This service generally costs around $100 per month and is worth every penny. The payroll service you select will also provide you with the necessary quarterly reports that your accountant will use to prepare your taxes.

Most insurance agents fail not because they do not know what is good or bad for business, it's because they fail to execute.

Do You Have What it Takes?

Most of us who studied management in college are familiar with Dr. Robert Blake and Dr. Jane Mouton's nine-panel grid which identifies behavior characteristics that are common among leaders. We have also seen numerous models measuring management skills and others that estimate sales ability. Although these models may be effective in one particular area, I have yet to see a grid that accurately measures a candidate's potential for becoming an effective small business owner. Just because someone is a great salesperson doesn't make him an effective manager of people. An effective manager isn't always a productive salesperson and many extraordinary leaders find it difficult to close a sale.

To help you determine if you have the potential to be a top-performing agent, I've created this very simple personality assessment tool that measures the characteristics every small business owner needs. Take a moment and see where you rank compared to successful insurance agents.

Insurance Agent Personality Assessment

(Check the box that most appropriately describes you.
Ratings: SA- Strongly Agree, A-Agree, N-Neutral,
D-Disagree, SD-Strongly Disagree)

Statement	SA	A	N	D	SD	Score
1. I have to finish all work before leaving the office for the day.						
2. Oftentimes, small details distract me from the big picture.						
3. I have a difficult time delegating work because I believe I would do a better job than anyone else.						
4. I prefer a commission-only position with high earning potential as opposed to a salary-based position with an acceptable steady income.						
5. I am the person to whom my friends and family turn in times of need.						
6. I effectively identify, analyze and solve problems.						
7. People who know me say I am comfortable with taking risks.						
8. The key people in my life support my interests and pursuits.						

Statement	SA	A	N	D	SD	Score
9. I do my best work when under pressure.						
10. I am a self-motivator.						
11. I am comfortable speaking in front of large groups.						
12. I have difficulty handling rejection.						
13. I often work late to finish a task.						
14. I often attend social functions.						
15. I have a positive attitude more often than not.						
Total						

See Appendix A to calculate your results.

Well, how did you do? Although this is not a thorough assessment and accurate predictor of success, if you scored low, I seriously recommend you do some further research and soul-searching before making this your full-time profession.

You undoubtedly know about the positives that owning your own agency can provide for you: flexible hours, unlimited income potential, challenging work environment and a career that allows you to help literally thousands of families. What I would like to do is cover the negatives, so you have a complete understanding of what you are about to get into. If owning your own business was easy, everyone would be doing it! Developing your own insurance agency is hard work. It takes countless hours, dedication, limited compensation early on and some capital to get it started... not to mention support at home. Let's look at each one a little closer.

Cash Reserves, Start-Up Expenses and a Whole Lot of Effort

Building a successful agency does not happen overnight. The key to financial success in this business lies in the renewal commissions. You have to work extremely hard for new business commissions, and you will not profit on a sale until the account has been in force for at least two years.

To begin an insurance agency, you should be relatively financially secure. As a general rule of thumb, you should have reserves to cover your growing expenses for the first six to twelve months. A new agent will not typically generate income from sales for three to four months. Most companies don't offer a compensation program early in their training program. The limited compensation is usually the primary reason people delay entering the insurance field until they are in their late thirties and early forties. If you don't have a large sum of money to draw from, look for a program that allows you to retain your current position until you are ready and committed to start your new career.

If the person interviewing you tells you money will come quickly, don't walk but run from his or her office. Insurance is not a get-rich-quick scheme. It is not uncommon for agents to spend 70 percent or more of their gross income during the first year to build their businesses. This business takes a few years to get started. If you need a large salary now, this may not be the best time for you to start your own business.

Early on, you will find yourself working non-stop trying to create your vision and build your model for success. Most customers have busy schedules and cannot see you until after hours and on the weekend. The long hours and weekend work make it difficult to balance your home life during business start-up. If you are expecting a normal schedule and a forty-hour work week, DO NOT START YOUR OWN BUSINESS! Many new agents lose sleep and weight in the start-up process. The good news is that if you do it right, this lack of sleep can be the result of excitement in developing your new career!

One of the most important but overlooked reasons agents fail in this business is an unsupportive spouse or partner. Because of the high risk, late hours, limited income and time away from home; many spouses do not share the same enthusiasm for the new business venture. I cannot emphasize enough how important it is to gain the support of your significant other *before* you start this career.

Here are a few ideas on obtaining your partner's support:

- Invite him or her to participate in the decision-making process.
- Allow him or her an opportunity to select the furniture or décor for your new office.
- Attend company functions together.
- Spend social time with successful agents who have "been there and done that."
- Keep your complaining about how tough it is to build a business to a minimum.
- Schedule lunch with your partner regularly.

- Prove to your partner you have what it takes to become a highly successful business owner.

- Always make time for your partner, letting him or her know that he or she is still the most important part of your life.

Making the Leap

Before you die, you will undoubtedly look back at your life and question the decisions you have made. You only have one life to live, and you need to do everything within your power to find out what makes you happy. If, after careful consideration, you decide that owning a business is not right for you, congratulations! Do not feel ashamed—you are not a failure. In fact, you have succeeded in determining what is best for you. Many people flounder a lifetime in careers that don't truly make them happy. Owning your own business is not for everyone. If you are not sure about what you want to do with your life, read Richard Bolles' *What Color is Your Parachute* to find some answers.

There is an incredible upside to this business. To name just a few:

- Our products are in demand.

- Most people are required to have insurance.

- We are paid commissions for many years after the initial sale.

- The average insurance agent earns just as much as the average attorney.

- The opportunity is great because many agents do a lackluster job of service after the sale.

Once started, most new agents find that it's actually easier than expected to create a successful insurance agency. If you are still excited about owning your own business after considering the options of an insurance career, it's time to take the next step and get started.

PART III

Getting Started

*Many of life's failures are people who did not realize how
close they were to success when they gave up.*

– Thomas Edison

So you think you can handle the negatives, and you are
ready to begin? The question now is: What type of agency should you own? In property insurance, two major agency systems of marketing are used to distribute auto, fire and
other casualty insurance: the independent agency system
and the exclusive (also known as captive) agency system. In
addition, there is a third type of system that deals directly
with the public. Independent agents are not affiliated with
a specific insurer. They are free to shop around and find the
best rates for their customers. Captive agents have a contract to represent a specific insurer. Let's look at all three of
these distribution strategies more closely.

Independent Agency System

In theory, independent agents have the consumer's best interest in mind. In reality, many independent agents get caught up in the price over service game and forget that price is not always the best option for the consumer. Financial stability of the insurer and making product recommendations have somehow been replaced in the independent world by "finding the cheapest price is always best" mentality. Independent agents who fail to understand that price is not always best find themselves with low customer retention rates and often lose as many customers as they write.

If you chose the independent agency model, it is extremely important that you find a General Agency that is supportive of you in your new career. It is a good idea to interview a few sales representatives with the firm before you commit your valuable time and money to the program. Becoming an independent agent can be quite difficult at first. Most insurance companies who broker policies through independent agencies require large sales volume to maintain agent appointments. Since most new independent agents cannot produce the required volume of new sales, many new independent agents actually become sub-producers for large general agencies. General agencies usually charge between ten to twenty percent of your total commissions for their services.

The benefit of opening an independent agency is being able to choose which authorized company to use. If one of the companies you represent is not competitive, you can simply shop around to place your policies with a more desirable carrier. Also when you decide to leave the business or retire, you may have the right to sell your agency on the open market. Finally, in a hardened market (where insurers tighten up underwriting guidelines to offset losses), the independent agent has more choices of companies to underwrite new policies.

The downside of being an independent agent is:

- You may need more employees to process the many new applications that are needed when you move customers between companies.

- You will have to understand the forms, applications and procedures of many different companies.

- You will lose your customers who seek brand loyalty.

- Since you are selling price over service, your customers will learn to shop for a better rate at renewal, which increases the need to constantly write new business.

Many of the independent agents I know are great people and truly believe they have the customer's best interest in mind when shopping for the lowest cost for the consumer. Sure, a home policy is a home policy, but companies can be significantly different. Often, it is not until customers file a claim that you find out they do not have the coverage they need or the company will not deliver on its promises.

Captive Agency System

In most cases, captive agents represent one or two primary companies. Like the independent agent, being a captive agent also has its advantages and disadvantages. The major disadvantage of being a captive agent is you are at the mercy of your carrier if the company chooses to stop writing certain types of coverage or is not competitive.

Very few captive companies offer a modified contract which allows agents to broker ineligible business. Even fewer allow you to transfer the agency to a qualified family member or sell it on the open market upon retirement. If you are going to choose this agency model, look for a captive company who allows you to broker ineligible business to an outside market, transfer your agency to a family member and receive compensation when you retire.

The advantages of being a captive agent include:

- Brand recognition
- Intensive training programs
- Financial incentive programs at start-up
- Ease of use (only one company set of forms, applications and procedures)
- Less work to service accounts
- A team of agents or managers to help you when you need it most

This is not to mention the personal relationship you form with the company of choice. If you want to develop personal relationships with your customers and offer advice-based sales, a captive agency may be your best choice.

Direct Writers

Direct insurance companies sell their policies to the consumer without an agent acting as middle man. Direct companies made their push in the marketplace as the Internet boom began dominating the media. Many corporations feared the worse believing that one day the middle man would be cut out of the equation—insurance agents were no exception.

The direct writing companies have captured a significant share of the auto insurance market over the past fifteen years with most of their new sales being made to a younger audience. However, in the May 2007 issue of *Insurance Journal*, a study conducted by Focalyst, a market research and consulting firm, showed that baby boomers remain loyal to a brand of insurance. The article went on to say:

> Baby boomers may be more likely to switch brands across a wide variety of products and services, including apparel, cars, prepared foods, and airlines, but when it comes to service oriented categories such as banking and insurance companies, boomers stay loyal to brand. Boomers are most loyal when companies give customized service…and are willing to pay more for value if a product or service demonstrates the ability to help make their complicated and stressful lives easier.

I don't believe baby boomers are much different from any other group of people. Younger people are more prone to shop on the Internet and choose price over service. When people get older and have more assets to protect, most will demand a relationship built on service instead of price.

Quite simply, people who use independent agencies and direct writers are shoppers. There is a reason why GEICO has an annual advertising budget of over $900 million! When you build an agency on price over service, your agency will experience high turnover as your customers shop for a competitive price on each renewal. Aggressive captive agents overcome this dilemma by offering value- added service at a competitive price.

Distribution Channel Summary

Thirty years ago, there was no argument about which type of distribution channel to choose. Because of the complex nature of our business most people prefer to purchase insurance from someone they trust. Captive agents ruled the market, and most policies were sold at the kitchen table. In the mid to late 80s, everything changed. With the Internet boom, insurance companies started jumping on the band wagon, promising discounted prices and faster service. Independent agencies offered to bridge the gap by shopping for the best deal for consumers while continuing to offer advice-based service. To survive, every company entered this price war looking for new ways to grow.

This price-instead-of-service trend is not specific to the insurance industry. Banks have begun treating us like numbers, computers are made to be disposable and, when calling most companies, the only way you can reach a live person is by going through an automated phone system and pressing zero fifteen times! The customer has somehow been lost in the shuffle. All of this has been done while, in fact, many consumers admit they would pay more to have good quality service.

When it comes to insurance, customers only shop with direct writers when captive and independent agents alike fail to provide advice-based service. Most customers want and need a recommendation.

Here is a chart that may help you make this very important decision regarding which distribution channel fits you. Keep in mind that if you have a family or dependents that rely on you financially, the most important factor in your decision-making process may be the ability to transfer your agency to a family member upon death or retirement.

Distribution Channel Benefits

Benefit	Independent	Captive	Modified Captive
Relationship-driven sales		X	X
Transactional sales	X		
Ease of doing business		X	X
Competitive pricing	X		X
Close relationship with carrier		X	X
Training and field support	Some	X	X
Brand recognition		X	X
Low service work		X	X
Transfer of agency upon termination	X	Some	Some

Making the decision on which channel and carrier to represent is one of the most important decisions you can make when entering the insurance business. While there may not be a right or wrong answer here, there are a few things you need to once again consider. First of all, you need to identify your target market. If your natural market niche is highly price sensitive when it comes to insurance, the IA channel may be the best option. If your target market is not as price sensitive and seeks a large reputable brand and are willing to pay more for quality service, the Captive or Modified Captive channel could be a better fit for your agency. Both are very good options to choose from and I highly recommend conducting a thorough investigation with both before signing a contract.

Now that you know which distribution channel is best for you, the next step is to research the companies that are in your local area and set up interviews.

Top 10 Writers of Property & Casualty Insurance By Direct Premiums Written, 2012

Rank	Company	Premiums	Market Share (Percent)
1	State Farm Mutual Group	2,594,199,070	10.5
2	Zurich Insurance Group (Farmers)	27,551,112,266	5.5
3	Liberty Mutual Group	26,658,767,630	5.3
4	Allstate Insurance Group	26,436,755,383	5.3
5	American International Group	25,324,099,724	5.0
6	Travelers Group	22,206,993,633	4.4
7	Berkshire Hathaway Group	17,956,557,684	3.6
8	Progressive Group	15,334,929,400	3.1
9	Nationwide Group	14,986,187,419	3.0
10	United Services Automobile Association (USAA)	12,125,537,473	2.4
Source: National Association of Insurance Commissioners (NAIC), 2012			

Top 10 Writers of Life Insurance
By Direct Premiums Written, 2012

Rank	Company	Premiums	Market Share (Percent)
1	Metropolitan Group	19,038,195,550	12.5
2	Northwestern Mutual Group	8,604,107,248	5.6
3	New York Life Group	8,238,947,555	5.4
4	Prudential of America Group	7,236,245,738	4.7
5	AFLAC Group	6,636,414,294	4.4
6	Lincoln National Group	6,215,779,646	4.1
7	John Hancock Group	4,933,448,569	3.2
8	Aegon US Holding Group	4,056,194,331	2.7
9	Mass Mutual Life Insurance Group	4,021,686,823	2.6
10	State Farm Group	3,705,904,525	2.4

Source: National Association of Insurance Commissioners (NAIC), 2012

Top 10 Writers of Auto Insurance
By Direct Premiums Written, 2012

Rank	Company	Premiums	Market Share (Percent)
1	State Farm Group	31,488,620,037	18.6
2	Allstate Insurance Group	17,451,278,899	10.3
3	Berkshire Hathaway Group	15,346,176,564	9.1
4	Progressive Group	13,423,204,913	7.9
5	Zurich Insurance Group (Farmers)	9,972,073,872	5.9
6	United Services Automobile Association (USAA)	7,778,763,692	4.6
7	Liberty Mutual Group	7,684,231,087	4.5
8	Nationwide Group	6,855,293,147	4.1
9	Travelers Group	3,526,738,412	2.1
10	American Family Insurance Group	3,042,992,183	1.8

Source: National Association of Insurance Commissioners (NAIC), 2012

Top 10 Writers of Homeowners Insurance
By Direct Premiums Written, 2012

Rank	Company	Premiums	Market Share (Percent)
1	State Farm Group	15,891,130,786	21.3
2	Allstate Insurance Group	6,972,557,667	9.4
3	Zurich Insurance Group (Farmers)	4,702,384,183	6.3
4	Liberty Mutual Group	4,088,561,071	5.5
5	United Services Automobile Association (USAA)	3,462,529,329	4.7
6	Travelers Group	3,441,895,660	4.6
7	Nationwide Group	2,743,125,634	3.7
8	Chubb Group	1,802,045,913	2.4
9	Citizens Property Insurance Corporation	1,567,340,653	2.1
10	American Family Insurance Group	1,531,338,055	2.1

Source: National Association of Insurance Commissioners (NAIC), 2012

Insurance Company Comparison Chart

Captive Company	Recruiting Office	New Business Commissions Auto Home	Renewal Commissions Auto Home	Deferred Compensation Plan	Transfer of Agency to Family
Farmers	800-FARMERS	10% 20%	10% 14%	Yes	Yes
State Farm	866-405-9813	Variable	Variable	Yes	No
Nationwide	Nationwide.com	12% 15%	10% 14%	Yes	Yes
Allstate	877-258-9012	3.5-10% 10%	3.5-10% 10%	Yes	Yes

Homeowners Insurance Provider Rankings

2012 National Homeowners Insurance Customer Satisfaction Survey by J.D. Power and Associates

5=Among the Best 4=Better Than Most
3=About Average 2=The Rest

Company	Overall Satisfaction	Policy Offerings	Pricing	Contacting the Insurer	Billing and Payment
Amica Mutual	5	5	5	5	5
State Farm	4	4	3	4	4
Nationwide	4	4	4	4	4
Allstate	3	3	3	3	3
The Hartford	3	3	3	3	3
Safeco	3	3	3	3	3
Liberty Mutual	2	3	3	2	2
Farmers	2	2	2	2	2
Travelers	2	2	2	2	2
MetLife	2	2	2	2	3

Auto Insurance Provider Rankings

2012 National Auto Insurance Customer Satisfaction Survey by J.D. Power and Associates
(Ratings vary by region)

5=Among the Best 4=Better than Most
3=About Average 2=The Best

Company (Region)	Overall Satisfaction	Policy Offerings	Pricing	Contacting the Insurer	Billing and Payment
Amica Mutual (NE)	5	5	5	5	5
USAA (Central)	5	5	5	5	5
State Farm (West)	5	5	3	5	5
GEICO (California)	4	5	4	3	5
Mercury (California)	3	3	4	3	3
Allstate (N. Central)	3	3	3	3	3
Liberty Mutual (NE)	3	3	3	3	3
Nationwide (Central)	3	3	3	3	3
Farmers (West)	2	2	3	3	2
Progressive (SE)	2	3	3	2	3

New Agent Program Comparison

(Captive Agent Opportunities)

State Farm

 State Farm is the largest writer of auto and homeowners insurance in the country, serving 80 million policies and accounts with 18,000 agents and 66,000 employees. To become a State Farm agent, you must complete the following eight-step process:

State Farm Agency Selection Process

Step	Description
1	**Assessment:** Complete a questionnaire called the Sales & Leadership Career Profile (SLCP). If you receive an acceptable rating, you move forward. If not, you may complete the SLCP again in one year.
2	**Overview:** You'll hear from successful State Farm agents and learn more about the company, how to become an agent, business support and compensation.
3	**Background Check:** This includes a standard review of your credit report, work history and motor vehicle record.
4	**Career Understanding:** During this web-based experience, you'll learn more about what it's like to be a State Farm agent and have an opportunity to connect with recruiting contacts and other agency candidates.
5	**Interview & Executive Approval:** During this panel interview with State Farm executives and agency field leadership, you'll submit your business proposal and share your strength and skills. If approved, you'll join the Approved Candidate pool.
6	**Posting & Site Interview:** As an approved candidate, you'll gain access to agent postings across the U.S. and Canada, where you may be invited to a site interview held by local management to select candidates for intern training.
7	**Internship:** Once selected for an internship, you become a paid, full-time State Farm employee. Intern training lasts six to nine months.

Step	Description
8	**12-Month Term Independent Contractor Agent:** Upon completion of your internship, you will become a 12-month Term Independent Contractor Agent (TICA). At this time, you'll receive a signing bonus and open your agency. After completing your TICA agreement, you'll sign the State Farm agent's agreement.

- **Time Line:** It takes approximately six to eight weeks to become an approved candidate. After being selected for a specific opportunity, the licensing and training process takes approximately six to nine months.

- **Type of Contract**: Captive

- **Starting Income:** Upon completion of Step 8, you will receive a signing bonus of up to $18,000 (amount varies by market). If required to move out of your local area, you'll also receive a lump sum relocation payment ($4,000 for renters and $10,000 for homeowners).

Allstate

Allstate is the second largest auto and homeowners insurance company in the nation and the largest publicly held property and casualty insurer with $125.6 billion in total assets in 2011. Allstate encompasses 70,000 employees, including 10,000 agents, providing coverage to nearly 16 million households.

To become an Allstate agent, you can either purchase an existing agency from an exclusive agent or build an agency from the ground up by following these steps:

Allstate Exclusive Agent Program Steps

Step	Description
1	**Review Program:** Review the program with an Allstate recruiter or field sales leader and complete a pre-screening evaluation. Familiarize yourself with the agency owner opportunity and complete the online Agency Selection Questionnaire.
2	**Begin the Process:** Meet with a field sales leader for an in-depth discussion of the agency owner opportunity and learn the differences between buying an existing agency and building a new one. Develop site selection options for your agency location. If you don't have your insurance licenses, begin this process immediately.
3	**Complete Requirements:** Complete a detailed financial review and your business plan and finalize all pertinent documents to ensure you are approved to become an Allstate Exclusive agent.
4	**Finalize:** Begin the education phase. Establish your agency location, interview and hire Licensed Sales Producers and begin generating sales and marketing leads.

To buy an existing agency, you must follow these additional steps:

- Work with your field sales leader to identify potential agencies available for sale.

- Begin negotiations with the seller to purchase the agency.

- Obtain preliminary approval to continue with the sale process.

- Determine if you need financing for the purchase and make these arrangements.

- Finalize the terms of the sale with the selling agent.

- Advise your field sales leader and complete the appropriate documents to gain final approvals.

You can find agencies currently for sale at Allstate.com.

- **Timeline:** Approximately three to nine months

- **Type of Contract:** Captive

- **Starting Income:** Education Bonus up to $6,500 (Varies by market)

Farmers Insurance (Zurich)

Part of the Zurich Financial Services Group, FARMERS Farmers Insurance Group of companies is one of the largest insurers of vehicles and homes in the United States. With more than 24,000 employees and 50,000 exclusive and independent agents, Farmers serves more than 10 million households across all 50 states.

In March 2000, Farmers acquired Foremost Insurance Company, adding mobile homes, motor homes, travel trailers and specialty dwelling policies to its product portfolio. In 2007, Farmers purchased Bristol West Insurance Group which allows Farmers agents the opportunity to write nonstandard automobile insurance.

To become a Farmers agent, you must first successfully complete the Farmers Reserve Agent Training Program.

Farmers Reserve Agent Training Program

Step	Description
1	Contact a Farmers District Manager in your local area to set up an interview or apply at BeAFarmersAgent.com. If you would like to hand select your mentor, a listing of District Managers can be found at Farmers.com.
2	Complete interview process with a local District Manager or authorized representative.
3	Complete background check.
4	Begin the training program part-time while you study for the necessary insurance license exams.
5	Once you pass the required exams and receive the appropriate product training, you become a Reserve Agent, which allows you to sell. If you are a top candidate, you may be selected to become a full-time Farmers Career Agent. All policies that you write while on this program remain in your book of business throughout your career.

Step	Description
6	Complete the three-year Farmers Career Agent Program while working hand-in-hand with your District Manager or in some areas, an Agency Support Center. This program assists agents with the fundamentals of becoming a successful business owner.
7	Attend the University of Farmers in Agoura Hills, California. Since its inception in 2004, this facility has been honored for its ground-breaking learning techniques and training excellence. Awards include five American Society of Training and Development Excellence in Practice citations, two Corporate University Best in Class awards, and the Pike's Peak for Excellence Award.

- **Time Line:** The approval process takes approximately two weeks. The Reserve Agent program usually lasts between four months to one year.

- **Type of Contract:** Modified Captive. Farmers Insurance agents are required to give Farmers Insurance first rights of refusal to all business. However, if the company refuses to insure the risk, the company may allow the agent to broker the policy to an affiliated Brokerage House or to another carrier all together. This contract also allows Farmers agents to transfer the agency to acceptable immediate family members upon termination or sell it to the highest bidder on the open market.

- **Income to Start:** Farmers Career Agents receive a subsidized income to help get them started in their new agency. The total amount is contingent on the success of the career agent and can total more than $75,000 during the first three years. Agents have the ability to waive the loan in full or in-part throughout the first three years of their career.

Nationwide

On Your Side®

Nationwide has more than $141 billion in statutory assets. The company started as Ohio Farm Bureau Federation in 1925 and relied on sponsoring Farm Bureaus to expand into other states. From 1943–1955, Farm Bureau expanded into twenty additional states and renamed part of its organization Nationwide Insurance. Today, Nationwide employs 36,000 people, has more than 16 million policies in force, and is the eighth largest property and casualty insurer in the United States. Eight Farm Bureaus continue to promote Nationwide and provide discounts to members.

To become a Nationwide agent, you must successfully complete the Agency Capital Builder Program.

Step	Description
1	Submit your resume to the corporate website. Your resume remains active for 12 months.
2	Interview with a Nationwide representative.
3	Work as a Nationwide employee for 18–24 months while you receive professional development training.
4	When you "graduate" from this program, you will get to leave with all your sales leads and compensation from their business.
5	Start your own Nationwide agency as an independent contractor.

- **Time Line:** Two years

- **Type of Contract:** Captive

Other Multi-Line Companies

Company	Where to Apply
Aflac	Aflac.com
American Family	Amfam.com
Farm Bureau	Apply online with your state specific company.
Liberty Mutual	Visit Libertymutualgroup.com and search for employee sales opportunities.
MetLife	Metlife.com
Mutual of Omaha	Mutualofomaha.com

PART IV

Your Vision for Success

The greatest business people I've met are determined to get it right no matter what the cost...the simple truth about the greatest business people I have known is that they have a genuine fascination for the truly astonishing impact little things done exactly right can have on the world.

– Michael E. Gerber

I want you to take a few moments and visualize your perfect agency. If you had an endless source of income...

- How many employees would you hire?

- What roles would each employee play?

- What would be your role?

- What would you focus on daily?

- Is there an agent who you admire personally and professionally?

- What sets him or her apart from other agents?

- How is this person's office staffed?

- What do you believe he/she has done to become so successful?

Take some time now to think about your business. If you fail to picture *your* perfect business, reading this book may be a waste of time. Pay attention here: You cannot construct the plan to get you where you want to go until you know what the end result should look like. To help you get started, let me tell you about one of the most successful business owners I know.

Learn From One of the Best

Gonzalo Jimenez

I am in the business of recruiting, training and coaching insurance agents to develop large insurance and financial service agencies. Over the past thirty years, my top agent, Gonzalo Jimenez, has built an insurance agency which provides service to almost five thousand households. During his tenure with Farmers Insurance Group, Gonzalo consistently finished the year in the top ten in life insurance production and in the top twenty-five in the issuance of homeowners insurance (out of 14,000 agencies). It is not his sales volume that impresses me the most about Gonzalo, it is the quality of life that he and his family have enjoyed while building this highly successful business. Let me explain how he does it.

Gonzalo employs fourteen modestly paid employees who are trained very well to do just a few tasks. Each employee has a clearly defined role and plays a significant part in the agency. Although he is the heart and soul of the business, he is not needed to make it run on a daily basis. As a matter-of-fact, Gonzalo would have a hard time answering a billing question or making a change to one of his customers' policies. In a sense, Gonzalo manages the people in his office who are responsible for carrying out the day-to-day activities of the office. Gonzalo enjoys a very financially rewarding lifestyle and because of his keen business savvy, he is able to take numerous vacations throughout the year, knowing that his office is in good hands.

What has Gonzalo figured out that many of my other insurance agents haven't? Gonzalo wasn't blessed with a silver spoon in his mouth. In fact, he grew up in Colombia, South America and came to this country with no money. He waited tables to make ends meet. Gonzalo did not purchase an existing agency. Instead, he worked hard to create one of the largest Farmers Insurance Group offices in the nation. Gonzalo, and his beautiful wife, Luz, figured out that people make your business successful. If you hire the right people, develop the right systems, clearly define each job and make each position as simple as possible, great things can happen. Gonzalo understood the value of a good employee. While building his company, he also took the time to build his people.

Your Organizational Chart

Now, create a rough sketch of an organizational chart for your perfect office. Instead of creating positions for your existing employees, think of your business functionally, as if it were an assembly line. This is an essential part of developing systems that are not reliant upon any one person. Most small business owners create their businesses around high-performance people. When those people leave, and in most instances they will, the business will suffer until another highly capable person steps in and takes over things.

Building a systematic process is an essential part of creating what I call a Level IV business. Take a look at the diagram on the next page. This organizational chart will represent your vision for your business and a progressive approach to achieving it. Use it to sketch out your Five-Year Organizational Chart. If you currently have employees, or know whom you are going to hire, place the name(s) of each person in the appropriate box. At this point, you may find yourself in many boxes. The key is to eventually have one person in each box. Now, ask yourself, "What can I do today to turn my vision into a reality?"

When creating your organizational chart, you must keep the basic fundamentals of management in mind. First of all, every business must be broken into to three distinct areas: Marketing, Operations, and Finance. Secondly, the span of control of each manager must not be greater than eight people.

To help you get started, the following organizational chart is what I believe to be a perfect insurance and financial services sales office.

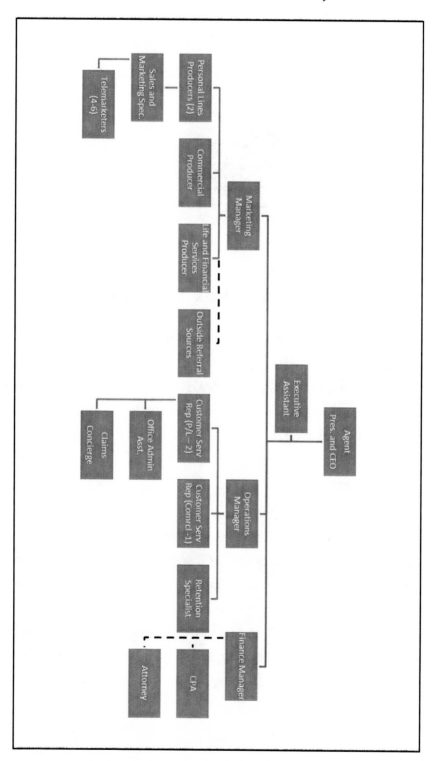

Out-of-the-Box Thinking

The opportunity for small business success in our country today is better than it has ever been. The many technological advances enable us to clearly define who our customers are, why they buy and when. Our success is only limited to our own creativity, talent and dedication to get things done. Of these three things, I believe creativity is what can set you apart from the rest.

A creative thinker is one who is truly an entrepreneur and a visionary. Business owners who can take what they are given and make it better will succeed. When faced with obstacles, they see an opportunity to succeed while others go home early. These business owners make things happen, while others wait for them to happen. They are leaders that others want to follow. They are visionaries who see past the obvious and look for new ways to get things done.

PART V

The Four Levels of Business Development

I've never known a man worth his salt who in the long run, deep down in his heart, didn't appreciate the grind, the discipline...I firmly believe that any man's finest hour – this greatest fulfillment to all he holds dear – is that moment when he has worked his heart out in a good cause and lies exhausted on the field of battle victorious.

— Vince Lombardi

In this chapter, I will share things I have done to consistently help insurance agents develop businesses that can help them live the American Dream without taking control of their lives.

It requires out-of-the-box creativity, flexibility and determination to get things done. Remember, if you want a Level IV business, then you must have Level IV thinking!

Why Most Agents Plateau

When I entered the insurance business, the typical captive property and casualty agent averaged around 1,295 policies in force (PIF). Today, twenty-eight years later, even with the technological advances that have made it easier to do business, the average agency size is has only increased by 10%. Are agents at this level simply happy with their income and are no longer motivated to work harder? Are they simply content? I've seen numerous agents take off out of the gate breaking all types of sales records and suddenly, for no apparent reason, stop growing.

After years of research and more conversations than I can count, I have concluded that most agents do indeed want to grow; they just can't figure out how to make it happen. Let me explain.

Most agents sell enough insurance until they create enough income to hire staff. They hire a new employee and keep selling until they can afford to hire another employee. Sell, hire, sell, hire. The business owner spends countless hours training a new employee only to find they fail to see a future in the agency and resign as well. "If I could just find an employee who wants to work," he says.

With only twenty-four hours in a day, eventually this agent will lose as many policies as he can issue and his agency will stop growing. Often tired and frustrated with his results, he looks to market conditions, employee performance and other factors to blame for his own shortcomings.

For most new insurance agents, when they enter the business, it took weeks, if not months, to learn how to rate an auto policy. By the time the agent was trained on the fundamentals of the business, which usually took well over a year, he was ready to get out of his manager's office as soon as the first renewals started coming in. Early in the business, the agent developed habits — some good, some bad. The service work started to pick up and he found little time to just keep up, much less time to work on his business plan. For this reason, he has created a stressful job instead of a highly functioning business operation.

It's not entirely the agent's fault! As an industry, we have failed to teach agents how to effectively run a business instead of just how to sell insurance. This comes as no surprise if you consider that the training programs today are very similar to the ones we used years ago. This point is extremely clear when you look at insurance companies that provide very little field management support. Many large companies have replaced experienced field managers with Human Resources Departments, leaving field training up to corporate employees who may have never been in business for themselves. While this type of training structure may be sufficient to train processing and product knowledge, it usually fails short when it comes to supporting an agent with running a successful small business.

Today, "rookie" agents are taught the fundamentals of insurance, how to process applications and, if time permits, how to close a sale. It is no wonder that captive agents and independent agents alike, who in many instances are in business for themselves for the first time, reach a certain size of agency and hit a brick wall. It doesn't have to be this way!

Choosing your mentor is just as important, if not more, than choosing the company to represent. It is in your best interest to interview with as many field managers as it takes to find a mentor who can help you succeed in this business. Your mentor should have the experience necessary to help you create a solid foundation for success.

So What Makes the Elite Agents So Unique?

How do the top 10 percent of agents grown to 2,500 PIF, the top 1 percent to 7,500 and the elite top ¼ of 1 percent grow to over 10,000 PIF? What makes the elite agents so unique? The answer is simple when you do the math: there are only twenty-four hours in the day and only one of you! If you know this and you want to develop a successful business, you have to create systems that do not rely on YOU being there to make them run.

Many people ask me the question as to whether or not having prior insurance experience is helpful before becoming an insurance agent. After careful thought, I truly believe that having experience can actually hurt more than it can help. It's agents that used to be CSR's that continue to do CSR work and fail to run a small business. If you have no experience, you are forced to hire someone that knows how to do the work which allows you to focus on building a business that works!

Highly successful agents think about their businesses in a different way. They create systems as if they were building an agency which could be franchised in many locations. When you create your business model with this in mind, everything changes! Your business is no longer being created with you in the center. If done right, your business will not be dependent upon your success as a salesperson.

Look at successful corporations today. Do you think any one of them would have ever taken off if the entrepreneur had failed to create a business plan, never developed an employee handbook or conducted employee reviews? Knowing this, why would you create your business any other way? Small business owners know this, but very few take it seriously enough to do anything about it. Now that you know why 80 percent of small businesses in America fail before the fifth year, do something about it!

Hastings Hierarchy of Business Development

As a Field Auditor, I had the unique opportunity to review and evaluate over 120 insurance agencies. During these audits, I reviewed not only their accounting practices, but also their production, business practices, employee duties and income. It was not until I left my position as an auditor and went into sales management that I fully understood how world-renowned psychologist Abraham Maslow's belief that humans must meet basic needs before they can satisfy successive higher needs related to business development. In short, self-actualization is reaching one's fullest potential based upon one's given circumstances.

Similar to Maslow's Hierarchy of Human Needs theory, I believe there are four distinct levels in small business development. To illustrate my point, let's look at Maslow's chart.

Maslow's Hierarchy of Human Needs

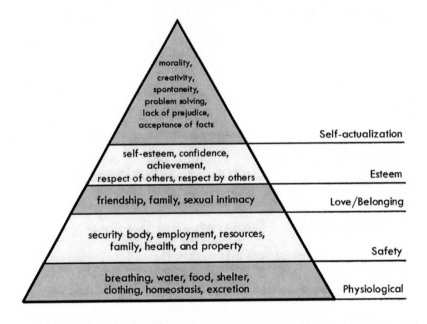

As you age and develop through time, there are certain needs that have to be met before you can successfully progress to the next level. Maslow believed if these underlying needs are not fully met, an individual would have a difficult time striving to be the best they can be.

I believe your business is a living entity in which the higher needs cannot successfully come into view and be met until the lower needs are satisfied. The lower needs represent the foundation of business development. Once all four levels are realized, you will achieve what I refer to as *Small Business Actualization*.

Hastings Hierarchy of Business Development

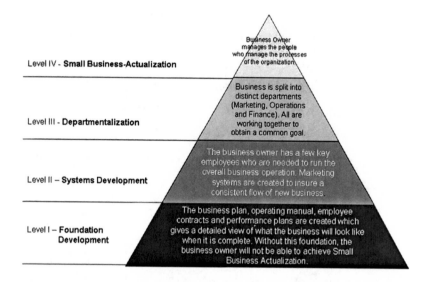

In order to reach a higher level, the business must first develop a strong foundation which includes:

- **The development of your personal and business objectives.** Define what it is your business is going to do for your life.

- **A well thought-out and structured business model.** Determine how your business will be structured to allow you to express your passion through your work.

- **A clear market strategy with a viable market segment for your product.** Understand who your potential customer is and why they would buy from you. What is going to make you different from everyone else?

- **A clear budget for your financial needs to get your business up and running.** Spend money on things that will make you money. When cutting costs, don't cut advertising and lead services which create revenue for your agency.

- **Written job descriptions for every position which will be filled even before the employees are hired.** Understanding this will continually be a work in progress, you should at least have the templates formed and ready to go which spell out compensation, benefits and minimum expectations. When you get this right, you will always be on the lookout for your next employee!

Each of these steps will help you create a blueprint for your new agency. Completing these steps is not easy and will take some serious effort; however, if you fail to do so, your business will undoubtedly take control of your life. The following traits are indicative of business owners who have created Small Business Actualization:

- They embrace the facts and realities of the marketplace rather than denying or avoiding them.

- They are spontaneous and quickly adapt to change.

- They are creative and see an opportunity in every market shift.

- They are interested in solving problems, and it is often the focus in their product development.

- They appreciate life and run their businesses rather than letting their businesses run their lives.

- Their businesses run by systems which are fully internalized and inter-dependent.

- They view all things in an objective manner.

- They spend 85 percent of their time on strategic initiatives and 15 percent on tactical ones. Tactical plans are carried out by the high level employees in the agency, freeing them to work on the direction of the business.

- They have less stress and enjoy the fruits of their labor because they are able to work on the part of the business they enjoy while leaving the work they dislike to subordinates.

- They take full responsibility for their own success and failures throughout their career.

- Their small business gives them the freedom to enjoy more life instead of controlling their life.

As a small business owner, it is up to you to determine where you are now and, more importantly, where you want to be. Let's take a closer look at each level as it relates to insurance agencies.

Level I: Foundation Development

There are four essential steps in building the foundation for your Small Business Actualization. Each step is interdependent and will change as your business matures. The failure to complete any of the steps noted below will make it difficult, if not impossible, to successfully move to the next level.

Step 1: Create Your Vision

As discussed in the previous chapter, you must clearly visualize what you want your agency to look like when it's complete. Every year I sit down with my insurance agents and ask, "Where do you want your agency to be in five years, and what are you going to do this year to get there?" I'm blown away by the number of agents who have no idea how to respond.

"This is *YOUR* business," I tell them. "As a business owner, don't you think it is extremely important to know what you are striving for?" They of course answer "yes," but because of bad habits, few veteran agents ever go back and complete the processes necessary to create a business that truly works. They continue, "You don't understand, Jeff. I've been in business for ten years, and I can't simply go back now and recreate all of the systems I have in place." Although this statement is not true, I do understand the complexity of the situation. In the following years, I find myself in similar conversations with the same agents, about the same problems and the same frustrations that never seem to end.

As a new business owner, I cannot overemphasize how important it is for you to complete all four of these steps early in your career. As you read this book, you should already be visualizing your perfect business. Once your vision is clear, you need to create your business plan so you can clearly communicate your vision to your team.

Step 2: Business Plan Development

Your business plan should be a living, breathing document that changes over time. During the early stages of your career, even before you write your first insurance policy, you need to construct the framework of your business plan. If your company does not provide you with one, I suggest you purchase a business planning software package to help you get started. I've provided a sample business plan for you to review in Appendix B.

Step 3: Business Differentiation

More than just being different, business differentiation identifies how your products or services consistently meet the needs of your target market. Insurance products are similar in nature. There are plenty of good companies out there, your customers are going to make their buying decision if and only when you identify their needs, present a solution to fulfill that need and deliver on your promise.

Think about your current perception of your insurance agent. What do you think they do all day? Do you look forward to visiting with them when the need arises? How often do they call you to review your coverage? Do they seem genuinely interested in your well-being or are they simply just trying to get your policy issued so they can earn a quick buck? Most people view their agent as a nice guy in a cheap suit, who likes to play golf, has a secretary named Sally and can be obnoxious when trying to sell you life insurance.

Let's face it, to most people, insurance is about as interesting as filing your income taxes. It's something they hate to do, but are forced to think about at least once a year.

So what can you do as an agent that could get prospective customers to change to your company? It's simply not good enough to know a lot about insurance. It's not good enough to be perfect and understand the in's and out's of how to get a policy issued. To be among the best, you have to find a way to totally and completely blow the socks off of the competition. The good news is it's not difficult to do!

Step 4: Define Your Marketing Strategy

Without an effective marketing strategy, you will not achieve success in this business. Developing your strategy consists of identifying your target market and defining how you are going to reach them. It's important to establish a marketing plan for every producer in your office and update it every year. You must be the Chief Marketing Officer in your business and set the expectation that marketing is something they must do routinely throughout the day. The type of internal or external marketing that is expected should be clearly defined in each producer's job description.

Internal marketing targets those who are already clients of the agency. Internal marketing includes:

- Selling multi-line discounts by offering the opportunity to quote additional lines of business,

- Mailing event postcards (e.g., birthday cards, anniversary cards, etc.), implementing an active referral program, and,

- Incorporating an annual policy review program for existing customers.

External marketing consists of programs which consistently bring in new customers. External marketing includes:

- Telemarketing

- Postcards and other mail out programs

- Newspaper, billboard, radio, Internet and television advertisements

- Networking

- Seminars

- Hosting local community events

- Developing an active referral program working with Realtors®, mortgage companies and auto dealerships

- Any other way you can get your name in front of prospective customers.

Internal and external marketing can also be broken down into two additional categories: *active* and *passive*. Active marketing requires you to ask for someone's business or meet them face-to-face. Passive marketing allows you to advertise, sit back and wait for your prospective customers to come to you. Active marketing will bring you clients fast, but will not give you an ongoing flow of clients.

While passive marketing brings in new clients more slowly, it will create an ongoing flow of clients. It is important that you utilize both marketing strategies. If you use only passive marketing early on, your business will fail or take years to develop.

Regardless of what your marketing strategy is, you must consistently run at least four active and four passive programs at all times! Document your strategy before implementing it with your producers, and be precise. It's not good enough to simply tell your staff to ask for referrals.

Be specific. Give each employee a script and a program to use. Develop a system to determine if your strategy is being carried out as planned. I will discuss more on marketing systems in Part VI: Creating Your Sales System.

Getting Stuck in a Level I Agency

When it comes to small business insurance agencies, I estimate that 25 percent are stuck in a Level I Agency. Unfortunately, developing the necessary systems can be a very difficult and time consuming process. Most business owners skip to Level II without first laying a strong foundation on which to build a business.

Agents who are stuck in a Level I agency are alone or have very few key employees. These agents are responsible for all aspects of their operations. They are recruiter, trainer, coach, motivator, customer service rep, and sometimes secretary. Most small businesses start out this way, and unfortunately, many stay this way.

These agents usually start off slowly because they rely on passive marketing programs early on and fail to invest wisely into their business. Although these agents usually feel they have put in a hard day's work, their day usually consists of putting out fires and answering calls from their customers. Because of their limited staff, they find themselves working on the urgent matters and having no time to pay attention to the important daily activities which will ultimately make them successful.

When they have "free" time, they use it working on paperwork or paying bills. An effective training program for their staff is almost non-existent, and employees often feel abandoned early in their career. Most employees usually admit the business owner does little to help them become successful, but expects them to get their jobs done. Because they fail to share their vision with their staff (if they have a vision at all) and rarely give employees insight into where they may have a future in the business, these business owners suffer as their employees leave for more secure opportunities.

The average production for a Level I agency usually dwindles because the agent usually finds it hard to generate enough income to invest back into the business. All of which could have been avoided if the business owner had developed the right systems, invested in quality people and developed a clear and focused strategy for the future. Because of the service work created in the insurance business, most of these agencies plateau at around 500–750 policies in force.

You often hear Level I business owners give excuses such as these for their failure to achieve positive business results:

- "If the company would only have competitive products to sell, I would be successful."
- "The agent down the street is successful because he cheats the system."
- "I live in a rural area."
- "I don't have the money to put into my business like other new business owners."
- "I was never trained."

- "My employees never seem to do what I ask them to do."

All of these excuses are a way for Level I business owners to rationalize their own failure to obtain positive business results. The truth of the matter is very few business owners have it easy during the early years of their career. Limited cash flow, no customer base and a lack of training make it difficult for most business owners to profit in the first few years.

Regardless of where you start, it is up to you to make the best of the situation. It takes a tremendous amount of hard work and creativity to grow a small business. What happens to your business is a direct result of your actions. Be accountable. Take control of your success!

In order for Level I business owners to take their businesses to the second level, they must:

- be accountable and take full responsibility for their success and failures.
- possess the belief that success is possible.
- have the dogged determination to do whatever it takes to make it happen.
- have a clear vision of what they want their businesses to become.
- have a clearly defined marketing strategy.
- develop a working business plan that clearly defines their business strategy.
- create an employee handbook and job descriptions which clearly identify the responsibilities of their staff.

Without a clear vision and a solid foundation, the likelihood of building a successful business is marginal at best.

Level II: Systems Development

When it comes to building a solid foundation for your business, the systems development process is an essential step that cannot be overlooked. Most businesses fail because they did not create systems to carry out the business owner's plans for future growth. In other words, if your idea of becoming an insurance agent is to obtain the necessary licenses, open an office, hire a few employees and market your product, your business will drive you crazy. Michael Gerber is known for saying, "The system is the solution," and he's dead on!

There are many types of systems: marketing systems, sales systems, cross-selling systems, referral systems, etc. Each system defines who you are as a business and how you differentiate yourself from the competition. Every business has a system, but until you write it down so that it can be easily communicated and understood by all who read it, you don't own it!

When developing your sales system, do your best to keep each process as simple as possible. Remember, you do not want to create a system that relies on a sales rep's talent to become successful. If you are fortunate enough to find a great sales rep, you can easily become dependent upon him to bring in new business. After becoming fully trained, the rep will undoubtedly venture out on his own and become an agent himself. When he does, you will be back to square one!

If you are a little confused, let me make it a little clearer. You do not need to find someone who has the talent to become your agency producer. Remember, you will be operating at least four passive and four active marketing programs at all times. Your passive marketing plans can be run by an internal marketing representative. Your external producers (working outside of your office) will work with mortgage companies and Realtors® to bring in referrals.

There is no need to show these producers how to close a sale or input an application—that is someone else's job! Training your sales producers on every aspect of your marketing program will take up valuable time and money, and you do not want to distract them from bringing in new business.

If you don't understand everything I'm saying here, please understand this: If you get an agency producer to stay with you for over a year, that's incredible! You are going to have to go through eight or nine people before you can find one who has what it takes to stick. Don't spend a lifetime training someone until they earn your valuable time.

Stuck in a Level II Agency

Some of my best agents are stuck at this level. Although they may be great at closing a sale, they are often controlling in nature and have difficulty releasing control to others.

They have tried to hire producers and became frustrated because the sales process was not completed in a manner acceptable to their standards. What these agents fail to recognize is that without a clearly defined sales system, there is not an agency producer on the planet who can read their minds. Often frustrated, Level II agents give up hope of finding that "key" sales producer and continue to be the one who is responsible for the entire sales process.

Level II agencies have one key employee and a few other clerical staff to help meet minimum goals. These agents may have a business plan, but seldom review it and spend little time updating it. Although they may have a clear understanding on where they want to take their business, they rarely share their thoughts with their employees, and they are unsure of their future. Employees are often unmotivated to achieve a high level of success and may take advantage of the lack of expectations required of their performance. Agents at this level feel there's just not enough time to get everything done and often become frustrated working on unproductive activities during the day.

Some of these agents develop very strong relationships with their customers and often spend time nurturing these relationships. These agents focus too much time on too few customers and, as a result, have limited time to market to new customers. Others spend too much time looking for new households and forget to develop the important personal relationships that are necessary to retain existing customers. These agents lose as many or more customers than they write new policies for because they are doing nothing to cross market to existing customers. Most Level II insurance agents feel pulled at both ends and can't do it all with a limited staff.

Unfortunately, over half of business owners fall into this category, and it's no wonder. Very few small businesses owners have a coach or mentor to help them get started. The owners rely on trial and error. When they first entered this business, they fell in love with the idea of being their own boss, but had no idea of what it really meant to develop a successful operation. "Opening up an insurance agency is easy," they thought. "People have to have insurance. All I need to do is open a store front location, hire a few employees and my business will flourish."

The product does not make a business. People can make or break a business. Without good people, you don't have a business — you have a job. Without systems that tell your people what to wear, how to act and what to do, you have chaos! If you ask any business owner what is the hardest part of his business, he will undoubtedly tell you that managing the people is the most important and the most difficult.

Level II agents effectively manage between 1,000–2,500 policies in force. To take a Level II business to the next level, business owners must:

- be accountable and take full responsibility for their success and failures.
- possess the belief that success is possible.
- have the dogged determination to do whatever it takes to make it happen.
- have a clear vision of what they want their businesses to become.
- have a clearly defined marketing strategy.
- develop a working business plan that clearly defines their business strategy.

- create an employee handbook and job descriptions, which clearly identify the responsibilities of their staff.

- hire key employees who know what their roles are in the business and are committed to the success of the operation.

Level III: Departmentalization

After developing your vision, creating your marketing strategy, clearly defining your systems development processes, and hiring six or more employees, you need to departmentalize your business operation. Your business operation should have three separate and distinct departments, Marketing, Operations and Finance. This is when your vision starts becoming a reality.

In order to departmentalize your operation, you must think of your office as an assembly line. Every staff member has a job to do in that assembly line if your product is to be complete.

Here an example of a sales system that is designed to support a marketing strategy in a departmentalized agency:

Marketing Department (Employee #1)

Implements marketing plans developed by the owner to make the phone ring.

Operations Department (Employee #2)

Answers the phone in a manner that is outlined in the operations manual.

Marketing Department (Employee #3)

Schedules and confirms appointments for customers to come in for insurance reviews.

Marketing Department (Employee #4)

Prepares proposals and delivers sales presentations. Asks for referrals.

Operations Department (Employee #5)

Submits policy applications and verifies accuracy of information.

Marketing Department (Employee #6)

Contacts clients every three months after a sale, then annually to come in and review additional lines of business.

Operations Department (Employee #7)

As Customer Retention Specialist, implements programs to make customers feel good about having insurance with your agency.

Granted you will not have seven different employees handling every function at first; however, this should be your ultimate goal. Creating a systematic process in your marketing strategy is the key to developing Small Business Actualization.

Stuck in a Level III Agency

It is not horrific to be stuck in a Level III agency. Only the top 10 percent of small business owners make it to this level, and even fewer make it to the next level. Level III agents have several key employees who are doing the right things to help their businesses succeed. They have regularly scheduled staff meetings and hold all employees accountable for their actions. Employees are on a performance-based pay scale and are motivated to generate revenue to add to the bottom line. Most of the employees in the Level III business respect their leader and believe they are supported and pushed to be successful.

Level III agents are high-energy, positive people who are always looking for new ways of doing things. They are eager to try new marketing programs and have a core group of employees who can be relied upon at all times. Since these business owners have developed a culture of successful selling, they usually have no problem meeting or exceeding their financial goals.

Constantly reviewing performance reports, Level III agents make strong efforts to work not only with developing new business for the organization, but with increasing retention of existing customers as well. Although they review goals often, they look at this as a minimum expectation and set higher standards. Level III agents are competitive and work to finish the year as one of the insurer's top performers. They usually win corporate promotions and, when their performance has been exceptional, they earn the company's highest honors.

Level III agents effectively manage between 2,500–5,000 policies in force. To take their businesses to the next level, the Level III business owners must:

- be accountable and take full responsibility for their success and failures.
- possess the belief that success is possible.

- have the dogged determination to do whatever it takes to make it happen.

- have a clear vision of what they want their businesses to become.

- have a clearly defined marketing strategy.

- develop a working business plan that clearly defines their business strategy.

- create an employee handbook and job descriptions which clearly identify the responsibilities of their staff.

- hire key employees who know what their roles are in the business and are committed to the success of the operation.

- establish clearly defined departments that work together to achieve a common goal.

Level IV: Small Business Actualization©

Finally, there is a level that very few business owners achieve, but all desire. We've all heard about it. A few of us have been fortunate to witness it. I call this Level IV business Small Business Actualization. In EMyth terms, we call this type of business, "E-Myth Mastery." In this business, all employees are working together to accomplish complementary goals. When you look at the organizational chart, the business owner is in one box at the top of the chart. These business owners manage the employees who manage the processes of the operation.

As owner, you are not needed for any process in the business. The business owner makes the high level decisions as to where the business is headed and develops the plan, but relies on others to carry out the objectives of the plan. Detailed organizational charts and an operations manual clearly identify how the business systems run. Departmental heads implement the plan in the manner designed by the business owner — every single time! No detail is left to question.

An amateur operations manual identifies such items as work hours and attire. Whereas a Level IV business owner creates an operations manual that spells out how each employee is expected to deliver an outstanding customer experience.

Employees are well trained, expected to perform at their highest level, compensated accordingly and supervised consistently. When these business owners travel, their businesses do not miss a beat. Level IV business owners enjoy a high-quality lifestyle and look forward to every Monday. Because Level IV business owners are not needed to carry out the operations of the business, there is no limit to the success they can achieve.

Where is your business today? Unfortunately, you can't jump to a Level IV operation overnight. You have to create it. It takes an enormous amount of work, money and creativity to make it happen. You have to be willing to pay the price, if you are to one day enjoy this level of success, and it all starts with investing in the right people.

Invest in Your Agency

It takes money to build a Level IV business. If you want to make your vision a reality, then you will have to invest in your business. A journey of a thousand miles begins with a small business loan. Early in my career, I had to borrow money and even charged up a few credit cards. I'm not proud of it. I just believed strongly in my decision-making ability and was willing to put the necessary money into my business to make it happen. Most successful corporations have to borrow money. That's why they issue stock. Instead of buying stock and investing in another company, invest in your own business and use it wisely.

You may have been blessed with a large sum of money as you came into this business, but most of us have not. If you haven't borrowed funds and are not independently wealthy, I would surmise that your business is probably average at best. If you consistently produce high-level results and have no debt, good for you! Please call me at the number on the copyright page and let me know how you did it. If you do not, don't be afraid to borrow the money needed to build your business. If you spend it on the right things, you can make your business grow and eventually pay off the debt.

PART VI

Creating Your Sales System

*No student ever attains very eminent success by simply
doing what is required of him: it is the amount and
excellence of what is over and above the required that
determines the greatness of ultimate satisfaction.*

— Charles Kendell Adams

In the insurance marketplace, it is essential that you adapt to fast-paced changes and take advantage of opportunities before your competition. Successful agents have one thing in common—they are dedicated to understanding the market place, not just today, but in the future. They are dedicated to finding out the needs of their target customer, what their perceptions are, how they think, act, how they make decisions and most importantly what would motivate them to take the time to purchase from them.

Knowing all of this is not enough; successful agents align their brand with their target market and have found a way to communicate how they can provide solutions to fulfill a problem that the customer may not even know they have.

The strategic work in developing the sales system is not the most important activity in your business, but it is the one that drives growth and income into your agency. It's the analytical side of your business development work and is vital to your success as a business owner.

The Sales System

A sales system is a set of processes and strategies that if done right, will generate the results you need to become financially successful. Your business needs a constant stream of new customers if it's going to remain viable. The constant churn in the marketplace, unless replaced by new customers, will cause your business to dwindle. If you are going to survive, you must find a way to bring in a large volume of new policies and develop systems to retain the ones you have. Without understanding these steps, you will find it difficult to succeed over a long period of time because your sales will depend on factors over which you have little control or influence.

An overview of the Sales System is shown in the following chart on the next page.

Step 1 – Identifying Your Target Market

Knowing who your target customer is and who is not is an essential step in your sales system. While demographics

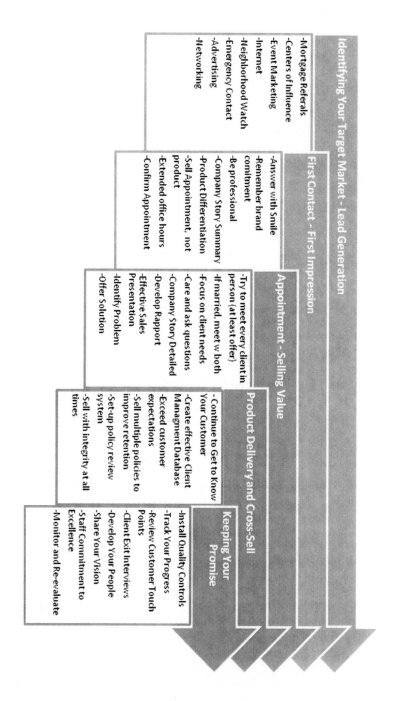

The Sales System—Building Your Brand

identify "who" your customer is, psychographics describes "why" they buy. Customer attitudes, perceptions of an insurance agent, and past experiences all play a part in the decisions they make.

Step 2 – Lead Generation

You should have 7-8 lead generation programs working at all times. Some of the most popular lead programs for insurance agents are working with mortgage companies, centers of influence, internet leads, referral programs, local advertising, business networking and community events.

Review your marketing message. Does the information give ideas or have an emotional impact for your target market? Does it grab their attention and prompt them to call? A summary of your company story or what makes you different should be advertised here to start building your brand in your community.

Step 3 – First Contact

Your brand promise starts the moment you answer your phone. From how your staff addresses your prospective client, to how they present an offer, you are being evaluated.

This is the first real touch point in your office. Evaluate how your phones are answered and how each call is handled. Do callers have to be placed on hold? Can proposals be done immediately or do you have to call them back? How quick are calls returned? Does the office staff sound organized and well trained? When collecting data from a potential client, does your message connect on an emotional level or are you just taking basic quoting information over the phone?

Step 4 – The Appointment

It may be almost impossible to meet every customer face-to-face during the first meeting. However, your sales system should require your staff to at least make an offer to do exactly that each and every time you prepare a quote. Just offering to meet clients in person makes you different than everybody else! Insurance is expensive—customers want your advice, but they may have perceptions that this type of old fashioned service is no longer available today. Successful agents are willing to do what unsuccessful agents are not. This is your opportunity to differentiate yourself and it is so easy to do. Now all you have to do is build a system around it.

Review your presentation material to see if your brand commitment is being communicated clearly. Is your packet professionally edited and printed? Give careful consideration to the layout and design of each piece to make sure you are connecting on an emotional level with your targeted client.

Step 5 – Product Delivery and the Cross Sell

Continue to document customer data in your data management system. I'm not just talking about knowing their address or they type of car they drive. I'm talking about really knowing your customer; where they work, when they got married, their children's names and what they enjoy doing for fun. Ask questions during the sales presentation and uncover their needs.

Don't be afraid to tell them your company story and why you opened your small business. Develop a "Top 10 Reasons to do Business with My Agency" list and hand it to them in your sales presentation. Always put the customer needs in front of your own, sell with integrity and earn their respect. Show that you have listened to their needs and care enough about them to spend the extra time to provide them a customized solution.

Step 6 – Keeping Your Promise

Keeping your promise means simply delivering on your brand commitment. Unless you are the cheapest insurer in the market, you had to sell yourself and why choosing your agency was the right thing to do was part of your sales presentation. You and your staff have undoubtedly made promises and commitments and it is up to you to develop the systems necessary to insure this promise is upheld.

Your business should be built on systems. Most agents have systems for attracting new business but very few have systems built specifically for policy retention and brand satisfaction. Build programs to insure an excellent customer experience at all touch points. And don't make all of your systems reactive waiting for your customer to call you. Develop programs that meet the needs of your best customers and reap the rewards of increased renewal commissions!

Your Target Market Explained

All too often, I see agents come into the business with no *real* target market or plan to reach them. And I understand. When you opened your agency, your target market basically included anyone who says, "Yeah, I'll buy insurance from you!" Well, this may be a necessary evil for you at first, but to sustain a long-term and profitable agency, a more structured and thought out approach will become necessary.

C.E.O. of EMyth, Jonathan Raymond and his team developed a lesson called *"Reaching the Right Customer"* (2012) which helps us understand our markets and identify our best possible customers. They help us focus our resources in the right places to attract the right customers, instead of scattering our marketing messages around hoping to attract anyone at all.

Raymond states, "The more strategic part of the marketing dynamic encompasses what is traditionally called market research—analysis which helps you understand how to segment your market, the demographics of your segments, and how to understand the personality, values, attitudes, interests, and lifestyles of your potential customers (psychographics). Once you've done the adequate research and analysis to help you choose the right channels and hone the right messages, marketing is primarily a tactical activity. You will want to systematize and schedule your marketing so that it takes place every day and every week; that way month-by-month you generate more leads that can be converted into customers."

Identifying your target customer may be harder than it seems. Sooner or later, you will realize that not everyone is the right customer. A good starting point is to first align yourself with a Company or model that fits in well with your values and vision for your agency. If your vision is to make insurance a commodity and sell price to your customers over the phone, you may fit in better by aligning yourself with the Independent Agency model. If your business and brand strategy is to offer advised based sales and offer the best possible product, you may fit in better aligning yourself with a strong and reputable Captive Agency model. This is not to say that IA agents can't offer advice or there are some captive agents who sell insurance as a priced-based commodity, but I think you get the picture. My main point is that you can become very frustrated in the wrong model where you are aligned with a company whose target customer is different from your own.

Attitude and Your Sales Performance

More than knowledge, more than desire, your attitude has more to do with your success than any other trait you possess.

Much of the art of selling is actually a combination of skill and attitude. Skills can be sharpened with practice and discipline. Your attitude is a much more complex animal to understand, but will affect your sales performance, relationships and, ultimately, your health if not checked on a regular basis.

Think about the last time you made a major purchase. How did the sales professional treat you? I would bet that the sales rep was very informative, seemed to enjoy his/her profession and had a positive attitude. On the other hand, have you ever dealt with a sales person who had a bad attitude? If you did, I'm certain you ran from him as fast as you could.

How can you change your attitude? Unfortunately, this is not a simple question to answer. Here are a few things I do on a regular basis to keep my attitude in check:

- **Spend time with positive people.** A positive attitude is contagious!

- **Get rid of the negative influences in your life**. Unfortunately, a negative attitude is contagious as well.

- **Don't worry about things that are outside of your control.** You can't change rates, your product offering or your competition. Once you understand this, you need to focus on how you can use what you have and be the best you can be.

- **Get excited about what you do!** If you don't like your profession — change careers. If you are simply bored, that's understandable. We all get bored. Hire a new employee. Change your office location. Learn a new product. Find a way to get that passion back.

- **Always try to see the best of every situation.** If you look closely, you will see that within every difficult situation lies an opportunity. Successful business owners realize this and capitalize on every market shift.

- **Do your best to walk away from gossip.** Gossip is usually negative in nature and filled with untrue rumors that can influence your attitude.

- **Make time for your family and friends.** You work hard so you can create a better life for you and your family. Never lose sight of this goal. Schedule time to spend with the ones you love and stick to the schedule. My oldest daughter is twenty-three, is a nurse and engaged to be married. It seems like only yesterday when I was teaching her to ride a bicycle. This is time you simply can't get back so enjoy every day like it is your last.

- **When you love someone, tell them.** I'm not just talking about your spouse or kids here. I once heard of a man who was dying of cancer and his comments have stuck with me for years. The interviewer asked him, "Now that you know you are dying, is there anything you would do differently in your life?" Without hesitation, the man replied, "Now that I know the end is near, I cherish every moment and when I love someone, I tell them." At that moment, I started to do the same thing. It felt funny at first hugging other men and telling them I loved them, but I got used to it. It's this love for mankind and appreciation for life that keeps your life in balance.

- **Don't hold grudges, and forgive those who have hurt you.** I have a long-time friend whom I haven't communicated with in years because of a petty disagreement we had years ago. Recently, I contacted him via e-mail to express my sorrow and apologized. When he responded with the same gesture, I felt a great deal of satisfaction knowing he knew how much I cared.

- **Write at least one thank-you card a week.** This reminds you to be thankful for your many blessings, and it may remind your friends and customers of how much you appreciate their being in your life.

- **Be thankful for what you have.** No matter how bad your circumstances may be, there is someone else who is worse off than you. If you doubt this, all you need to do is volunteer at the local children's hospital or burn center. Just spending a few hours in one of these facilities will make your problems pale in comparison. It will also remind you to appreciate every day.

- **Limit your intake of alcohol in times of depression.** Short-term depression after a negative occurrence is normal. On the other hand, long-term depression can have a dramatic impact on your well-being. Alcohol is a depressant and should not be used if you are battling depression. Seek the assistance of a professional if you can't seem to get out of a rut.

- **Worship in good times and in bad.** Having faith is the only solution for many people who seem to have problems that are out of their control. Like many people, I pray more when times are tough or when I need God the most. Whatever your religious belief, having a personal relationship with your God can keep you focused on what is really important in life.

Maintaining a positive attitude, a willingness to help others and excitement for the products you sell is a must in any sales profession.

You Never Get a Second Chance to Make a First Impression

From the moment a customer or prospective sales rep walks into your office, you are being evaluated. Take a moment to walk through the door of your office and try to see it as a customer might.

- Is the office clean?
- Are your employees' professional, fun spirited, full of energy and eager to help?
- Is your sales packet professionally printed?
- Does it explain what makes you different from your competitor down the street?
- Do you know what makes you different from your competition?
- Take a few minutes now and write down your thoughts as to what is going to make your agency different.
- What encourages customers to purchase insurance from you, even if the price is higher than the competition?

Let's face it; in this business, it's not the product that makes you different from your competition. It's your commitment to knowing your customers and delivering on your promise that makes you stand out from the crowd. Great service does not mean that you get it right when your customer calls to add a new car to his auto policy. You must develop systems that blow the socks off of your customers' expectations! Your customer expects that you meet their needs. Give them more than they expect and show them the value for doing business with your agency.

Be proactive. Call your customers before they call you. Go the extra mile. In the end, facts really don't matter, but perceptions do. Do what direct writers can't do and what other agents aren't willing to do which is meet them in person, listen to their needs, uncover gaps and unnecessary coverages and make a product recommendation to fulfill their needs. Yes, I've already mentioned that once and I may do it again before you are finished reading — it's that important!

Branding

Create a personal brand that differentiates you from other agents. Tell your personal story and elevate your marketing message and materials to create maximum marketing leverage.

When you hear the word "branding", you may think of your Companies logo, slogan or jingle. But what I mean here in terms of branding is your own personal message that you would like to communicate to your target market. Your brand is what your customer's perceptions are of your agency. It's why they buy from you or why they leave. If your customer perceives your agency to be the best, worst, cheapest, most expensive — regardless of whether or not it is true or not, their perception is their reality.

If all you do is piggy back off of your Companies logo and quote price every day, your brand is that of a commodity seller where price will be king. You may be able to get away with this if you always offer a cheaper product; but when you don't, you will undoubtedly suffer and potentially fail in this business.

When determining your brand strategy, you must take a close look at every step of your customer contact point. Some of these customer contact points include: advertising material, website, emails, color selection, office appearance, employee appearance, phone etiquette, bills, claims handling, customer service and sales process to name a few. From the moment of first contact, your prospects perception of your brand is being formulated and influences their decision to buy or to pass on your product.

To create a favorable brand image, you cannot leave any stone unturned. It takes time to develop and determination to see it all the way through. Even after fully developed, you must continue to monitor, change and improve upon your brand.

"It takes a lifetime to build a reputation and only 15 minutes to destroy it."

— Warren Buffett

At EMyth, they believe like trust, favorable branding must be earned over time. The EMyth philosophy believes you should take the time to create and write down a Brand Commitment Statement[1]. The Brand Commitment Statement:

- Provides the why to the way you do it
- Keeps you customer-focused and creates customer loyalty
- Is your competitive edge
- Differentiates you
- Integrates culture and customers

Social Media

I remember how excited I was when I purchased my first personal computer in 1986. It was a Compaq 286 with a 5.25 floppy drive and 1 megabyte of memory! I majored in Computer Information Systems and used, even built, computers before...but this one was mine and I couldn't wait to open the huge box, put it together and connect to the World Wide Web. That night, it seemed like forever for my wife to get off of the phone so I could connect. But when I fi-

---

1   *EMyth Foundational Lesson* – the Brand Commitment offered through EMyth.com (2012).

nally did…Ah, the sound of the computer connecting to the Prodigy on-line service; it seems like only yesterday!

My friends couldn't understand why I would spend $2,000 (over two-months income) on a personal computer because back then, computers were considered for business use. I found myself explaining to people on a regular basis what I actually used it for and even had a boss tell me that he believed personal computers were a fad that would soon disappear. I thought he was so old and outdated. I loved being on the cutting edge of technology and known as the guy who understood where it was all going. Technology changed at a rapid pace. It seemed as if as soon as you got your computer home and took it out of the box another faster processor was developed or a larger hard drive was created.

And here we are today over 25 years later. But instead of being the one with all of the answers and understanding where everything is going, I'm the old man who thought social networking was for kids and Facebook was just another sophisticated gossip board. Somehow, without me realizing it, I went to sleep and woke-up as a technologically challenged ex-computer nerd who couldn't tell the difference between a hashtag from an Instagram.

Over the past 10 years, I have spoken about, written about and often publicly criticized insurance agents who relied on technology to run their business. In the insurance industry, I felt the technology weakened the relationship between the agent and the customer and if we were going to survive, we had to get back to the basics, get out of the office and go see our clients. Although I continue to believe this today, I had no idea how using social media could improve relationship selling; that was until I met Angela Johnson and Nadeem Demani.

In their book *Going Tradigital* (goingtradigital.com), Nadeem and Angela show us how to bridge the gap between traditional relationship selling and technology. They showed me the power of social media and the possibilities to use avenues such as Facebook, Twitter and YouTube to reach an audience of thousands, if not millions, to create a buzz about our business which can potentially bring us more customers than we ever dreamed possible.

Although I found myself behind the curve when it comes to using social media, the good news is it's not too late for me, and it's not too late for you! Using the techniques mentioned in their book, you will undoubtedly increase sales, improve retention and build a stronger relationship with your customers who you are privileged to serve.

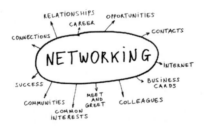

Working with Realtors® and Mortgage Companies

In our business, being in the right place at the right time can greatly increase our success. When you purchase a new car, you can simply add the new vehicle to your existing auto policy. However, when you purchase a new home, you are required to apply for a new homeowner's policy.

Why go after one household when you can go after someone who can send you ten? Developing relationships with local Realtors® and lenders will get your business off to a quick start. We all know that referrals are a major source of income, but too many insurance professionals don't realize how many referrals slip past them as missed opportunities.

There are great programs out there to establish relationships with Realtors®, mortgage companies and title companies. Quickbinder.com, clientfocusconnections.com and RECAMP.com are among the best.

Leads

If you browse through and run a Yahoo search for insurance leads, you will find almost 6,000 different companies trying to advertise how their lead service will somehow answer the age old question, "How do I find more quality prospects?" I'm exaggerating of course, but there are a so many lead services it is important you can cut through the clutter to find one that works best for you.

In the case of buying leads to help grow your agency, it is true that you get what you pay for. The lowest cost leads (pennies per name) is simply a name and a phone number. A moderately priced lead ($2–$5 per lead) is usually sold to 4–5 different agents who will compete for the business. A higher priced lead (over $10 per lead) will be a pre-qualified "hot" lead and may only be sold to one person. I recommend that you spend at least twenty-five percent of your total budget on lead services early in your career and a minimum of $500 monthly.

If you don't know where to find the best lead service in your area, simply search for "insurance leads" on the Internet and a list of hundreds of companies will appear. All of them will be eager to sell their services to you.

Regardless of where you purchase your leads, it is imperative that you don't simply use the lead to prepare a quote. You are a professional insurance agent who takes the time to explain policy benefits and coverage. Don't short change your customer!

Stop Quoting and Start Giving Proposals

We have to get back to the philosophy captive agencies were founded on years ago: to offer superior, customer focused, advised-based service. In years past, this type of service was the norm in most industries including the insurance and financial services world. However, in this fast paced technology driven age we live in today, most agents have lost sight of this and have become process-driven machines that rely on our competitive position to grow. Subsequently, they lose policies as quickly as they issue them. The key to long-term success is relationship-based selling.

When your customers hear a commercial from one of your competitors, they think of you. When one of my agents complains to me that they lost a customer to a direct writing insurance company because of price, I simply ask, "Well tell me, what reason did you give your customer to stay? The direct writing company didn't contact your customer directly to offer a competing quote. Your customer contacted them. If all you do is quote policies and sell on price, your customers will leave on price. It's that simple! Offer value, give your customers a reason to stay with you and they will never pick up the phone to get a competing quote."

Don't quote rates over the phone. I know, some of you are now thinking I'm crazy and have no idea of the real world. Well, if I'm wrong, don't tell one of the most successful female agents in the country. Pippa Wiley of Houston, Texas, has been an agent for more than 20 years and has qualified for her company's highest honors (President's Council) every year of eligibility. Because the state of Texas has almost 4,000 agents and only takes less than twenty-five to this prestigious event, I would say that is an outstanding achievement. On many occasions, Pippa has come to my office to speak with new agents or hosted my rookie agent meetings in her office.

Pippa believes meeting her customers face-to-face made her the successful agent she is today. She taught my agents a script several years ago that our Customer Service Representatives (CSR) still use. It is printed here with her permission.

CSR: Good morning, Farmers Insurance. This is   . How may I help you?

Customer: Yes, I wanted to get a quote for homeowner's insurance.

CSR: That's great! How did you hear about us?

Customer: My Realtor® gave me Pippa's name.

CSR: Oh, are you new to the area? Is this your first home? What does it look like?

(Use a little personal chat to start developing rapport with the prospective customer.)

CSR: Mrs. Johnson, we are so happy you called and would love to be your insurance agent. But first, I need to tell you a little about Pippa and the way we do business in our office. As a professional insurance agency and want to make sure you have the coverage you need — no more, no less. The only way we can make a professional recommendation is to find out about you and what it is that you need to protect. The only way we can do this is to take the time to ask you a few questions about your home and liability needs.

I will give your information to Pippa and I can schedule an appointment for her to come out to give you a proposal on what she recommends for you and your family. When was the last time an agent had this type of interest in you?

Customer: Well actually, I don't think my agent has ever done this for us.

CSR: I hear that a lot. Most agents you call will simply give you a quote without really knowing what type of coverage you need. Is that the type of service that you would like from your insurance agency? (If the answer is no, Pippa states that she closes almost one hundred percent of the time. If the answer is yes, don't waste your time. The prospect was most likely not interested in changing agents, but was merely shopping. You just saved your staff twenty minutes.)

Pippa's selling approach has allowed her to have one of the highest retention ratios in the company. She also has the highest number of policies per household, and the highest number of umbrella policies sold across our entire sales territory. In 1999 and again in 2013, she was named the Property and Casualty Agent of the Year.

It's the Relationship That Makes the Difference

Most agents make the fatal assumption that all of their customers are highly price sensitive. They design their marketing program with that idea in mind. When they are the cheapest carrier on the block, more people buy. When they are not the cheapest, fewer people buy. Although price can be a reason for customers to switch, you may be surprised by the primary reason people make buying decisions.

When it comes to insurance, there are two types of buyers: *transaction-driven* buyers and *relationship* buyers. Transaction-driven buyers are only interested in the cost of protection for each purchase. These buyers have no loyalty. As soon as they find a cheaper price, they drop you as fast as the next policy can be written. They spend hours on the Internet researching before they buy. They take pride in getting the best deal. Direct writing companies and a majority of independent agencies market to these customers.

Relationship buyers are looking for an agent they can trust— agents who recognize them, remember them, and build a relationship with them. They are seeking friendly agencies with a financially credible carrier. Once they have found such an agency, they tend to give them all of their business. They know that they could save a few bucks here or there by shopping around, but they find the process wastes too much of their time and energy. Relationship buyers, if properly cultivated, will stay with you for a lifetime.

Look for common ground on which to start a relationship. To help you remember this extremely valuable sales technique, remember the acronym S.C.H.O.O.L. when selling to a relationship buyer.

SELF: People like talking about themselves.

CHILDREN: Next to talking about themselves, most people enjoy talking about their children.

HOBBIES: Do you have common interests in sports, cars, boating?

OCCUPATION: Try to find friends in common. This link can help turn a cold lead into a hot prospect!

OBGYN: This one doesn't really fit; I just wanted to see if you were paying attention.

LAUGH: No matter what your conversation may entail, always try to have fun and laugh. Without laughter, this life would be extremely boring!

Building an agency by marketing to the relationship buyer makes all the difference in the world to a captive agency. In this business, it costs a lot of time and money to close a sale. All too often, you actually spend more money to obtain a new client than you actually earn in commissions. Selling a policy takes time and money, but the renewal commissions will make you wealthy. Policies that lapse before the second renewal will ultimately cost you. You must find ways to market to relationship-driven customers and nurture these relationships throughout the year.

Keep Your Relationship Buyers Happy

Your average transaction-driven buyer will stay with you approximately 9–18 months. These buyers usually have a different agent for their auto, home, life, health, business and financial services.

Relationship buyer's value having one or two agents who handle their entire insurance and financial service needs. Statistics show that if you add one additional line of business to a mono-line household, the customer will stay in your agency for 4–7 years. If you add life or financial services to an existing mono-line household, the customer will stay with you for 11–13 years! Keeping your relationship buyers happy is crucial to your long-term success. The key to keeping relationship buyers happy is selling based on *relationships*. The way to do this is to:

- **Know who they are**. Keep track of them in a database. Ask relationship-driven questions when preparing a proposal for insurance. Enter relationship data into your database. Birthdays, anniversaries, special interests and children's names are great ways to get started. Treat your VIP customers like VIPs. (More on this in a moment.)

- **Don't wait for them to call you**. In most agencies, the owner relies on indirect servicing to satisfy his customers' needs. When a customer calls to complain, they get serviced. When a customer calls to inquire about a new policy, they get a quote. The problem with this indirect servicing method is that your best customers seldom call, so your worst customers get your best service.

- **Communicate with them**. Find special ways to build a relationship with them. Thank them for their business. Contact them at least seven times each year in a positive way. Don't let the bill they receive from you be the only reminder of who you are. Secure Corp (www. securecorp. net) is a great program many of my agents use to thank customers for their business and invite them to come in for an annual review.

- **Use your best customer service people**. If your Customer Service Representative is having a bad day, get her off of the phone! If she has many bad days, put her in another position or terminate her. In this business, answering the phone with a smile is a must!

- **Don't quote apples to apples**. Most insurance agents do a poor job of recommending coverage options. If you quote apples to apples, you are relying on someone else's work and opening yourself up to a lawsuit for failing to make an appropriate product recommendation.

- **Only refer the best**. Whether it's a car repair center, fire restoration service or rental car agency, always refer your customers to the companies who will deliver top quality service.

I'm not sure who said it first, but I love the quote that "Successful people are willing to do what unsuccessful people are not." In the insurance world, most agents are willing to do whatever is necessary to find a customer, issue a policy and do as little as they can to service the client when needed. I sincerely hope you will not become one of those agents. Maintaining a high retention ratio of your best clients is paramount to the success of your agency and doing this can be as simple as doing the little things that matter most to them.

To give you an example of what I'm talking about, on August 2, 2006, I sent a birthday card to a dear friend of mine that I hadn't seen in a few years. Her name is Julie and we used to car pool in the late 80's to our job in Austin, TX. She is seriously one of the sweetest people I have ever met in my life.

Although I'm not exactly certain what happened when she opened the birthday card; I can assume she was a little confused because her birthday is actually in September. When she called me, she was obviously shaken up as she was crying telling me how much she appreciated my gesture. On August 2, 2006, Julie had been cancer free for 5-years. Her struggle with breast cancer was a difficult battle but Julie had actually forgotten the date. The card cost me about $1.50 and took less than 15 minutes to create on-line. It's the little things that often mean the most.

Value Selling

Like it or not, before you approach a target customer, they have a preconceived idea about who you are and what it is you have to offer. From their point of view, talking about insurance can seem like a blessing and a curse. Of course when they have a claim, you quickly become their best friend! But before that time, most consumers would rather clean the garage. They have been here before. And not just with insurance sales representatives.

Many view sales people as pushy, high pressure, say anything or do anything just to make a sale. Nobody likes a pushy salesperson and hopefully, you will not build your agency like one. On the other hand, if you go in with the strategy to help others and focus on the clients' needs, you can quickly overcome this negative perception.

Today's insurance agents have become product peddlers. They offer a product, sell it and wait for the customer to contact them if they have a problem. For years, I have taught new agents to sell value and to stand out in the crowd of relationship challenged insurance agencies in the market today. All too often, most of them get caught up in the volume game, focusing on the transaction rather than the relationship. A few see the big picture and capitalize on it.

Value-selling agents sell three things—the product, the company and themselves. The give the customer the information they need to make an educated decision and peace of mind. Let's face it, people buy from you, or refuse to do it primarily for one reason alone—they either like you or they don't. Since there are many good insurance companies to choose from, and most products are similar, the agent is the one selling point that stands out from the rest. Here's how:

- Value-selling agents do not quote rates over the phone. They use the phone to make appointments to meet prospective customers in person.

- Value-selling agents do not sell insurance policies. They offer solutions to fit their customers' needs.

- Value-selling agents do not go on sales calls. They go on job interviews with prospective clients.

But new agents please understand this: some clients really like you and even your product but will refuse to buy. The reason for the hesitation is simple and has nothing to do with you. This reason may only be the fact that you are new, you have no staff or not enough experience for them to trust that you will be in business next year or even next month!

Changing insurance companies takes effort and many potential clients, and even family, may hesitate buying insurance from you in the early phases of your career. But they will never tell you that to your face. Instead, they will tell you that your price is high or make up a story that their agent is a relative before telling you that they just don't feel comfortable switching to you at this time.

So how do you overcome this? Invest in your agency, get an office and hire staff. If you are on a very tight budget, get an executive suite and hire a high school senior to intern at your office. Once you've made the leap into owning your own business, you have to think like a business owner and that requires an investment of your time and money.

The Multi-Policy Sale (Cross-Sell)

For those of you who select the multi-line agency program, you will have the opportunity to provide many types of products and services to your customers. This is a huge sales advantage over those who only offer one or two products.

Many multi-line companies also offer discounts to customers who purchase multiple policies from the same company. These discounts make the products more competitive and can ensure there is no duplication or gaps in your customer's insurance coverage.

My most successful agents package policies in every sale. They sell the customer on the benefit of having one agent take care of all of their insurance needs. Developing this personalized service builds relationships that last even when the rates are not the most competitive in the market.

Trade Shows and Special Event Marketing

Trade shows and event marketing refers to specials events in your target community which helps you create or improve brand awareness. Sponsoring community activities, holding seminars or setting up booths at a sporting event can be a great way to meet a large amount of people in a short amount of time. But be careful, if you approach this wrong or are not prepared, conducting this type of event can be a costly mistake. To maximize your dollar, here are a few tips to help you avoid these costly mistakes:

- Be prepared and have enough support staff to handle the table/booth at all times. Events like these can be expensive. Your goal is to meet as many people as possible, gather information and get agreement to meet with them at a later date. Some will want a quote immediately and that is great! Just make sure to have licensed support staff with you at all times. You don't want to miss a big sale because you didn't come prepared and one person asks fifty questions about why he is paying too much for car insurance.

- Test your technology before the big day. You don't want to have technical problems like a poor internet connection the day of the event when you really need a good internet connection to do what you need to do.

- Spend a little money on your booth or table and make sure your message advertises your brand commitment. Remember, you should try your best to connect emotionally with your target audience. If you do it right, your target audience will want to walk up to your booth and to find out more. Also, you make look a little silly sitting at a plastic table and a stack of business cards when your competitor is close by with a display booth and free ice cream for the kids.

- Have giveaways or something to attract people to come see you. A roulette table with prizes is always a big hit with a nice prize as one of the gifts. Require them to complete a contact card to spend the wheel. Also, hand out big bags with your agency name on it to carry around other trinkets being given away at the event. Kid prizes are usually inexpensive and a huge hit at family events.

- Prepare in advance. Don't wait for the last minute to pack your table and order trinkets only to find out you don't have what you need to have a successful event.

- If it sounds costly, pair up with a partner agent and split the cost. Working these events are fun and it's always nice to have someone to share the energy with.

The Extremely Important Life Sale

Out of Every 100 People
25 are dead before reaching age 65
71 are financially in need at age 65
4 are financially independent at age 65

U.S. Department of Health and Human Services and actuarial tables.

An interesting way to look at the table above is that 96 percent of people either die too early or they outlive their finances.

The role of an insurance agent is never more important than when it comes to protecting a family against the financial hardships that come after the loss of the head-of-household. You may be the only person who brings this need to the attention of your customers and that alone is a tremendous responsibility. Your goals as a life insurance professional are to (1) help your clients discover and accept their financial needs and, (2) encourage them to act now to satisfy those needs.

Helping people meet their needs means first bringing the specific financial or emotional needs to their attention. Life insurance can:

- fund final expenses resulting from death

- replace lost income

- allow the surviving family members to maintain a certain standard of living while mourning the loss of a loved one (e.g., not having to sell a home or forcing the children to change schools)

- finance higher level education

- pay estate taxes

- provide continuity and security for a family business

Unlike selling a home or auto policy, unless the policy is tied to a business, people purchase life insurance because of love. Life insurance is an emotional sale. For this reason, it is extremely important to involve both partners (if applicable) in the buying process. Agents who have never experienced the benefits of life insurance first hand usually look at it as just another product to sell. When one of your customers dies, and they will, knowing you have failed in some way will hurt for a long time. Let me tell you a story about a friend of mine who experienced this lesson the hard way.

An Example - Henry Gomez

In 1996, Henry contacted me a few days before we had an agency development meeting. His request was a bit odd and vague to say the least, but Henry asked a favor of me. He said, "Jeff, do you mind if I talk to the agents in our district about a few things during the district meeting? All I need is five minutes." Hearing the tremble in his voice, I didn't interrogate him and agreed to his request.

On Thursday, after a brief introduction and opening re-
marks, I informed the group that Henry wanted to say a few
words. Although Henry was a relatively new agent, he was
very respected by his peers and liked by everyone. A little
nervous, Henry came to the podium.

Guys, it's hard for me to talk about something, but I really need to tell you about what
just happened to me. Last week, my best friend
was shot and killed for less than $200. You
may have read about it in the paper, but if you
didn't, let me tell you the story. David worked
sixty hours or more a week at a local convenience store trying to make ends meet for his
wife and four kids, all of whom are under ten
years old. On Sunday night, some punk kids
robbed him and as they were leaving, one of
them shot David twice before they drove away.
I keep asking myself,

'Why did they have to shoot him? They already had the money!'

Needless to say, he didn't have any life insurance. Sure, I'd asked him about it. I knew
he needed it, but he always insisted that on
his income, he just couldn't afford it. For the
first time in my career, I realize the importance
of what I do for my clients. (Henry started to
cry.) It is killing me knowing that I could have
done a better job. Please don't let this happen
to you. From now on, if I see a customer who
has a need, I don't care if they buy from me or

someone else, but I will drag them down and
beg them to buy from someone!

There wasn't a dry eye in the room. To this day, Henry has a copy of the newspaper clipping framed above his desk to remind him of his responsibility. By the way, David's widow had to sell their home and move her children into an apartment in a nearby town. What a tragedy!

Cross-Selling Made Easy

I've talked a lot about creating processes in your business instead of relying on any one person to handle it all. Most agents make the mistake of asking their current employees to cross-sell (sell multiple policies in each household) without giving them the tools they need to generate positive results. More importantly, most agents don't create the systems to validate if the cross-sell attempt was even made by the employee.

There is a simple solution that will insure that your CSR asks for the cross-sell at every opportunity. This solution requires that you ask for information on your customers' existing policies with other carriers on every quote request. It's that simple. If you are quoting a home policy, ask who has their auto policy and the renewal date. Require your CSR to write it on the quote sheet. If you give your CSR a nice bonus for every cross-sell she makes, she will be excited to ask for the business!

What we Learned from Pavlov and His Famous Dog

If you studied psychology at any point in your life, you are probably familiar with Russian scientist Ivan Pavlov and his famous dog. While studying digestive reflexes in dogs, Pavlov made the discovery that led to the beginnings of behavioral theory. He could reliably predict that dogs would salivate when food was placed in their mouths through a digestive reflex called the "salivary reflex." Yet, he soon realized that, after time, the salivary reflex occurred even before the food was offered. Pavlov continued experimenting with the dogs, using a tone to signal for food. His results matched. The dogs began salivating when they heard the tone.

That's great Jeff, but what in the heck are your talking about? What does Pavlov's dog have to do with my insurance agency? It's simple actually. Our responses to certain activities are a direct result of prior experiences. It is human nature to create habits. Our employees will undoubtedly create habits in our work environment as well. It is up to us to make certain their work habits are productive and generate the results we want. It is much easier to teach a new employee your new sales techniques than it is to ask an existing employee to change his or her processes after they have developed conditioned responses in your office environment. Here is a simple example that illustrates my point.

Creating a Sales System Example

Would You Like Fries With That?

"Would you like fries with that?" is a simple question that has made one fast food restaurant millions of dollars. Even more amazing is the average sales person is under eighteen years old! This sales system transformed the fast food industry and virtually every chain now uses a similar technique for success.

Just as McDonald's mastered the art of packaging products through combo meals and asking for additional business, you should also use this sales technique with every transactional sale. Quote homeowners' insurance with every auto policy, and vice versa.

Here is a great script that I've taught CSRs for years. After gathering the correct information to properly quote the homeowners policy, simply have your CSR ask the following questions:

CSR: "Would you like mortgage protection with this proposal?"

Prospect: "What is that?"

CSR: "Because your home is probably one of your largest assets, if something happened to either your or your spouse it could be very difficult to pay off your mortgage. Mortgage protection will pay off your mortgage in case of the death of you or your spouse. It is not the best type of protection in the world, but it's better than nothing. If you like, I can include it in your proposal, and you can let us know later if you want it."

I used a label maker to print "Do You Want Mortgage Protection With That?" and placed it on every CSR's phone. This script is also printed on our homeowner's quote sheet. By creating a simple system of asking, we uncover many sales opportunities that would have gone undetected.

In addition, each staff member is required to have the customer who rejects this protection to sign a "Life Insurance Declination Form" and keep it in the customer's file (See Appendix I).

Using this form is a way to validate your system. You can tell your employees to do it, but if you have no way to measure it, most employees will fail to ask when you are not around. One of my agents has even gone to the extent of placing a bell in his office. Every time employees fail to ask for the additional line of business, a co-worker rings the bell. Employees who do not ask for the additional line of business are forced to put $1 in a bucket. At the end of the month, the employee who has scheduled the most appointments to discuss life insurance keeps the money. Now that's creative!

Women and the Buying Decision

Men, wake up and pay attention to this section. In her book, *Prime- Time Women* (trendsight.com), Martini Barletta indicates that women are the CPOs (Chief Purchasing Officers) at home and in the workplace. They control more than 80 percent of all consumer purchases and represent more than half of the corporate buyers. Marti goes on to state, "It's no secret that men and women have different communication and decision making styles as well as different priorities and preferences." When it comes to insurance matters, I would estimate the number to be significantly higher. Knowing this, you should always review your marketing material and sales style to cater to the female buyer.

To target female buyers, you must first put yourself in their shoes. What issues are they most concerned about, and why? How are women and men different when it comes to relationship sales? How can you change your sales presentation to fit the needs and desires of the female buyer?

Women face an increasing problem of outliving their partners. Many women have the difficult responsibility of maintaining the home and family if they are widowed earlier than expected.

Currently, over half of the women who are over age seventy-five and do not have spouses live in poverty and are looking for ways to stretch their income over a longer period of time. Whether you are male or female, you must find ways to use your expertise to help guide your female clients through the issues of estate planning to a prosperous future.

Most women dislike aggressive sales tactics while most men prefer to have a quick and simple explanation. Men believe what they hear, women believe what they read. Men are often quick to make a decision while women want all of the information to make an educated choice before they buy. Men usually prefer to make transactional sales while most women prefer to develop a relationship with someone they trust. If you make it your goal to *educate* your female prospects and not to *sell* them, you will gain their trust, their business and their referrals.

Always remember when meeting with a couple it is important to equally include both of them in your conversation because they will compare notes after you leave.

Stop Cold Calling

Get Three Referrals with Every Sale!

Let's face it, cold calling is not fun. Unfortunately, you may have to spend a lot of time on the phone if you don't have a large network of friends to tap into early in your career. If you hate to cold call, you had better get great at asking for referrals.

Most sales reps simply hand out cards asking for referrals. Although this feels productive, 99 percent of their business cards end up in the trash. A better way to get referrals is to ask for three names from your new clients, close friends and family members of people who may be interested in your services. Of course, the best way to get referrals is to develop a systematic way of asking that is done with every client by every employee every time. Two great examples of this are the Emergency Contact and Neighborhood Watch programs.

Emergency Contact Program

It is a good business practice to ask for an emergency contact with every customer account. When you ask for the name of someone to contact in case of an emergency, you will receive a name and phone number almost 100 percent of the time. Here is a script you can use when you call the emergency contact.

CSR: Hello, Mrs. Rodriguez. This is Jeff Hastings. I'm Martin Gomez's insurance agent. How are you this evening? I'm sorry to bother you, but I needed to let you know that Martin has listed you as his emergency contact. What I would like to do is mail you a magnetic business card for you to keep on your refrigerator. Let's hope nothing ever happens to Martin or his home when he is away, but if it does, would you please call me to let me know about it? You may call twenty-four hours a day. My home number and my cell phone number are printed on the magnet in case you need to call me after hours. By the way, even though I'm not your insurance agent, if there are ever any questions you have about your own insurance products, please feel free to call me at any time.

Neighborhood Watch Program

Similar to the emergency contact program, the Neighborhood Watch Program is a great way to obtain the name, phone number and addresses of two or more of your clients' neighbors to use as a contact in the case of an emergency. This is a great way to generate warm leads as it provides instant rapport with a trusted neighbor. To make it work, you must contact the neighbors by phone and ask for permission to mail them a magnet to keep in a handy location. Keep these prospects in your database, and continue to market to them on a quarterly basis.

Call Reluctance

Call reluctance can rear its ugly head in several ways. It not only affects cold calls, but also prospecting. From getting your hair cut to meeting a waiter at your local restaurant, you must prospect at EVERY opportunity. Put the three-foot rule into action: anyone who gets within three feet of you gets a business card! Expect the people who accept your business card to return the favor. This is so simple and obvious, yet I am amazed at how relatively few people do this. I attribute this problem and the fear of picking up the phone to call reluctance.

According to Exceptional Sales Performance (exceptionalsales. com), twelve types of call reluctance impact telephone and face-to- face selling.[2] The types of call reluctance that are most relevant to our industry are: over-preparing, stage fright and telephobia.

Over-preparing occurs when you over-think how to obtain a sale, yet under-act due to stress. According to Exceptional Sales Performance, over-preparing results in closing only 43 percent of sales quotas. A salesperson suffering from *stage fright* usually fears public speaking and loses an estimated $10,800 in sales per year. *Telephobia* is the fear of telephone prospecting, which can cost a salesperson up to $10,000 in new business commissions every year (not to mention renewal commissions)[3].

---

2   Connie Kadansky, "12 Types of Call Reluctance," www.exceptionalsales. com (accessed December 13, 2007).
3   Jacques Werth, "Eliminate the Fear of Cold Calling and Rejection," www. highprobabilityselling.com (accessed November, 2007)

Everyone who prospects experiences call reluctance from time to time. Although there are many reasons for fear, the reasons for call reluctance can be divided into two distinct categories: repeated failure and rejection.[4]

The first reason for call reluctance is the fear of *repeated failure*. This occurs when you attempt to schedule appointments with all the contacts on a prospect list and are repeatedly turned down. Each time you fail to schedule an appointment, the next contact becomes harder to complete due to the increasing fear of failure.

The second reason for call reluctance is the fear of *rejection*. When you call to schedule appointments from the contact list, you will usually ask a series of questions from a rehearsed script. Often the prospect becomes defensive, negative or refuses to talk with you over the phone. The fear of rejection may stop you from prospecting.

Reducing call reluctance depends on your type of call reluctance. For example, one way to cure over preparing is to make sure you leave the office by a certain time in the morning. This cuts down on the amount of time you have to prepare and actually start selling for the day. If you suffer from stage fright, one solution is to practice in front of a group of peers on a regular basis. Doing so will help eliminate your fear of public speaking and improve your prospecting skills. Secondly, reducing call reluctance demands setting realistic goals. [5]

---

4   Carroll, John. 2002. "How to Overcome Sales Call Reluctance," www.uper- form.com/articles/art-reluctance.htm (accessed August 10, 2007)

5   "Overcome Sales Call Reluctance With Exceptional Sales Performance," www.exceptionalsales.com (accessed August 14, 2007)

One way of eliminating the fear of repeated failure is to measure success by the number of scheduled (not unscheduled) appointments on the contact list. You can help eliminate the fear of rejection by understanding that it is the product or service that is being rejected, not you.

Being unable to overcome call reluctance is detrimental to your career. If the problem is left unresolved, it causes frustration and loss of sales and income.

Why Customers Leave

Most insurance agencies have little to no idea why customers leave them when they do. When you ask most agents why their customers leave, you will often hear, "Because of price." The truth is: Your customers will typically leave you for one of the following reasons:

- They die or relocate to another territory.
- They are unhappy with the price.
- They are unhappy with your product.
- They are unhappy with the way they are treated.

In most instances, we blame the price when we know the customer lives in the same house and did not complain about the product we have offered them. However, research shows the most common reason customers leave is they are unhappy with the way they have been treated. Specifically, they leave because either the agent failed to return phone calls promptly, or the agency staff failed to properly make the requested changes to the customer's policy.

Whether or not your customer is a transactional buyer or a relationship buyer, if you fail to deliver excellent service and nurture the relationship after the sale, your customer will find a better price or service with one of your competitors. Your customer purchased a product from you which means he accepted the price and the product. If a customer leaves because of price, you must first ask yourself, what did we fail to do that prompted our customer to pick up the phone and get a competing bid?

Develop a system to find out why your customers leave your agency (See Appendix H: Exit Interview). Some of the customers you want back. Some you would love to send a postcard from a competing company so they will leave! You need to know which customers you want back and continue soliciting them to return to your agency. If you don't do this, your customers will rarely come back, even after they determine leaving you was a mistake in the first place. Take away their embarrassment and continuously work to win business back into your agency.

Practice Field Fridays

Get out from behind that desk, and go see somebody! Just like many of you, I often get overwhelmed with paperwork and urgent (but not important) work on my desk. Meeting with your customers face-to-face will improve your attitude and remind you how important you are to the customers you have insured. Your customers need you and want your attention. Give it to them!

Hire the Right People

As soon as a man climbs up to a high position, he must train his subordinates and trust them. They must relieve him of all small matters. He must be set free to think, to travel, to plan, to see important customers, to make improvements, to do all the big jobs of leadership.

— Herbert N. Casson

When you open your door, you need to have at least one part-time employee. This employee should bring in revenue and quickly generate profit in your agency.

Most importantly, this employee will allow you to do the thing you need to do to grow your business — sell — without spending time on the routine service work. In my experience, the best agents hire early and often.

Recruit the Right People

If you are like me, you will admit that you have made hiring mistakes and you don't know why. The candidates meet all your entry level requirements, they seem motivated and skilled, yet when it comes down to selling, they just don't perform to your expectations.

One of the key things I have learned during the past fifteen years of interviewing and hiring sales professionals is this: no matter how good I am or how much service I provide, the most successful sales reps would have been successful with or without me. In other words, being able to develop the art of spotting talent and hiring the right people is one of the most critical skills you must develop to run a successful agency.

According to Deloitte Research, organizations today face an acute shortage of critical talent with the necessary skills to drive above-average business performance. In a 2004 Accenture High Performance Workforce study, 70 percent of executives rated improving worker productivity as a top HR priority, but only 6 percent said they were "very satisfied" with the progress in their organizations. As a result, companies face a new imperative to improve employee productivity and talent management.

Because we allow emotions and feelings to enter into the equation when predicting future performance, when interviewing future employees our personal observations are not enough. Observations may be part of the picture; however our judgment may be skewed with prior incorrect evaluations and our assumptions could be a far cry from reality.

Take a moment to look back at the people you have recruited. What characteristics set the great reps apart from the not-so-great? I have found that the best sales reps have one characteristic in common. It is not their education or how much they know about my business. The great ones all have a burning desire to succeed. This internal passion to succeed makes great sales reps unique. You must find a way to spot this talent during the first meeting, looking for inherent characteristics that will help you predict future success and behavior patterns.

Although I have to admit that I have not tracked the qualifications and performance of employees that I have hired over the years, I am meticulous about tracking every insurance agent I've ever interviewed. In an effort to improve my interview skills and select the right person for the position, I track 12 different traits and attributes of each candidate during the initial interview. And if the candidate turned insurance agent is successful after the two-year benchmark, the agent information is automatically moved over to a separate spreadsheet which gives me an idea of what to look for in my current interviews.

With 15 years of data, what I have found to be the most relevant traits for a commission based sales rep to be are, 1) they had lived in our community for five years or longer, 2) their family supported their interest in starting an agency, and 3) they started on our training full-time rather than part-time.

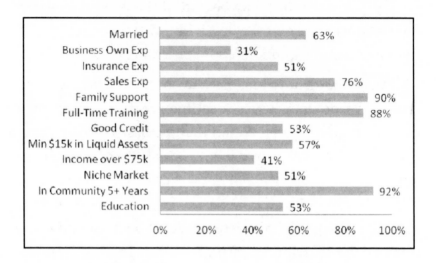

Here are some additional qualities you should look for:

- Is the candidate competitive?

- Does she demonstrate desire, drive and set goals to become highly successful?

- Does she believe in the products you sell?

- What type of research did she conduct about you and your company before coming in for the interview? Or, did she do research at all?

- Is the candidate leaving her prior position on good terms? Ask about every position on her resume. Ask about her responsibilities, the training program and specifically ask why she left. Look for positive or negative indicators.

- Why is she looking for a new position today?

- Is she confident in her own abilities and open to trying new ways of doing things?

Make certain your advertisements attract candidates who have the characteristics of your top performers. Often we use ads that state: "A college degree or management experience required." A potential top performer may not even respond. On the other hand, if you would have advertised that you are looking for candidates who "have a proven track record of prospecting," you may attract aggressive candidates who are willing to do whatever it takes to become successful.

The following stories describe a few of my personal hiring experiences. Perhaps they will help you understand what to look for in a sales rep.

An Example - Jorge Gonzalez

In July 2001, a young man by the name of Jorge Gonzalez walked into my office for an interview. Although I had met him once or twice before when he worked for one of my agents, I didn't remember him. My top agent recommended I meet with him and said he was a very hard working, ethical person. At first glance, I wasn't impressed by his appearance. Don't get me wrong, Jorge is a good-looking guy, he just wasn't your typical polished salesman. To this day I believe he bought the tie just for the interview. He didn't meet all of the requirements necessary for my opening, but I loved the guy. Jorge had passion. I could see it in his eyes.

Jorge told me about his life growing up in Mexico where he sold lollipops on the street corner. His mother wanted a better life for her children and brought them to Texas in 1982 when Jorge was just eleven years old.

During the interview, Jorge asked me to please give him a chance. He promised that I wouldn't regret it. Well, it's been twelve years now, and I haven't regretted hiring him for one second! In just a short period of time, Jorge has grown his agency to over 2,500 policies-in-force (PIF) and consistently produces over 80 life applications per year.

In October 2007, Jorge became a US citizen. Today, he is married, has two beautiful children and has just purchased the home of his dreams. Now if that isn't living the American dream, I don't know what is!

An Example - John Smith

John came into my office about the same time as Jorge. John was one of the most polished candidates I ever hired. He was an attorney and graduated from one of the most prestigious law schools in Texas. John was looking for a change. He had a network of friends who were eager to help and had already lined up four sales producers to work for him before his second interview. Any agency manager would have loved to have the guy in their operation and would have jumped at the opportunity to hire him.

John had it all. His family provided a nice life for him and paid for his college education. Although he was extremely intelligent, John looked for the shortcuts in life. He was a visionary and had the right idea of hiring people, but he failed to put in the hard work up front to create the systems to develop a business that truly works. Also, while he was excited about the opportunity to make a lot of money, he was not passionate about running an insurance agency. Five months after completing the training program, I had to terminate John for failing to produce the life results necessary to stay in the program.

What made Jorge different from John? John was the perfect candidate while Jorge could have been turned down due to our entry level requirements. It was Jorge's work ethic, passion and desire for a better life that set him apart. It is this passion that I look for during the interview process.

Before you or your office manager sits down to interview a candidate, you must understand that every prospect will have one or more of the following traits: detailed, controlling, driven, passionate, competitive, empathetic, confident, positive outlook on life or have a need to be nurtured. Let's look into these characteristics a little closer.

- **Detail Oriented:** Many engineers and accountants fit this profile. While a detailed individual can become successful, this person will usually start off slow and will miss many opportunities to close a sale. A detailed person usually has to know everything there is to know about the product before he or she can begin the marketing process. While a detailed individual may not fit well in a sales role, he or she may fit well in an administrative role in your office.

- **Controlling:** Many detail-oriented people are also controlling and want to make certain that each process is handled in a certain manner. Although a controlling individual can become a superstar sales performer, he usually has a hard time delegating work and at one point, his business will stop growing.

- **Driven/Competitive and Passionate:** These qualities set most top sales performers apart from the rest. Without the internal drive combined with a passion for success, the chances of success will be marginal at best.

- **Aggressive Personality:** Most successful sales reps are aggressive. Submissive candidates often find it difficult to close a sale and have call reluctance.

- **Spousal Support:** I've seen many quality candidates fail simply due to the fact that they had an unsupportive partner at home. In a commission-based position, there is often a delay in receiving the financial rewards for your hard work. When finances are tight at home, this often leads to a very difficult transition to a performance based position.

- **Empathetic:** Sales reps that are empathetic develop stronger relationships with their clients and their employees. The ability to understand the attitudes of others is a tremendous asset in the sales profession.

- **Confident:** A sales rep who is not confident in his or her ability will have a hard time facing rejection and may be better off finding a comfortable job that does not rely on performance-based pay.

- **Results Oriented:** Prospects who set goals and focus on results often have a higher performance than those who do not.

- **Positive Outlook:** Although I've seen some very negative top performers, I would rather take less income and hire an average sales rep with a positive attitude. A negative person can bring down an entire team. Fortunately, this is the trait that is easiest to spot during an interview.

- **Need to Be Nurtured:** This trait may not make or break an agent; however, I thought it was worth mentioning because this type of sales rep will require more of your attention than most. People who have this trait need your constant attention, and they need to be told they are doing a great job.

Online Profiles to Select the Right People the First Time

World renowned author and management guru Peter F. Drucker once stated, "All organizations now say routinely, people are our greatest asset. Yet, few practice what they preach, let alone truly believe it."[6]

This statement cannot be further from the truth as evidenced by the number of business owners who continue to recruit new blood into their businesses without first making certain the prospect fits their corporate culture.

In 2001, I hired an experienced outside sales rep to sell life insurance and financial services. For the sake of privacy, I will call him Jimmy. As always, I interviewed six to seven people before I hired Jimmy and even had him complete

---

6   *Classic Drucker: Essential Wisdom of Peter Drucker from the Pages of Harvard Business Review* by Peter Ferdinand Drucker, page 147.

an extensive online profile before he was contracted. He was sharp, very well spoken and extremely professional. Jimmy had worked for a life-only insurance company and appeared to do very well. I thought he was the perfect candidate. The online profile did not agree. The profile recognized that Jimmy had a hard time accepting instruction and a tendency to be negative. The report also indicated he would not work well on a team. My staff met with Jimmy and agreed with my recommendation. I hired him after the second interview.

Nine months later, Jimmy had run off two very good employees and several others threatened to do the same. I couldn't believe it. How could this guy interview so well, and why couldn't I see it? To this day, I have no idea how much this mistake cost me in the long run. My advertising and recruiting expense alone cost me well over $3,000. I personally spent about 120 hours training Jimmy. I provided an office and a six-month guarantee of $4,000 per month to get him started. This doesn't even take into account the loss of two good employees, the deteriorating morale in the office, lost sales opportunities and lost time! If I had paid attention to the online profile, I would have avoided this hiring nightmare.

Today I use an on-line profile from www.chequed.com. For a small monthly fee, this profile allows me to screen an unlimited amount of candidates. In addition, the automated reference checker requires the candidate to input three referrals. The referrals not only help me determine if they are right for my opening, the referrals could be possible candidates for insurance or even for a position within my sales team.

Develop an Effective Recruiting System

There are two types of business owners: those who are successful and those who are not. Failure to attract and retain high quality people will ultimately lead to your own demise. If you are to become successful, recruiting cannot be a part-time activity. It must be a systematic process that you work on every day.

Whether you realize it or not, you have a recruiting system. It may be good, or it may be bad, but you have a system. The question is: Does your recruiting system generate the results you want? If the answer is "no," you may want to pay particular attention to this chapter.

I've used the Insurance Learning Institute (insurance-learninginstitute.com) to better train and prepare my staff to excel in an insurance career. The institute specializes in insurance training programs, state licensing preparation and insurance specific sales programs. Just recently, ILI has added recruiting systems into their program giving insurance agents in the State of Texas access to a group of prepared and licensed insurance professionals who are ready to work.

Developing an effective recruiting and training system is an essential part of your long-term success. To understand your recruiting system and to determine where it's broken, you must first review your own results. You will need to track your interviews, new hires, employee terminations and employee success.

Invest in Quality People

In order to keep up, we must have an extremely capable, motivated, and creative staff to assist us in this process. Many agencies have staffs that are large enough to sustain, but too small to grow. As a rule of thumb, not including yourself, you will need at least one staff person for every 150 households to grow your agency. If you have a large number of automobile policies, you may need slightly more. Spend money on staff. There is no substitute for well-trained, highly motivated employees. It is better to have a few great employees than many not-so-great ones. It will cost you more up front, but it will pay off in the long run.

Like many of you, I find it hard to keep up with the numerous changes presented to us on a daily basis. Hiring a quality staff is crucial to your success. As an effective business owner, you must lead your people who manage the processes. Our job is simple: Hire the right people, and teach them the right things to do.

As most of us are unfortunately aware, an employee with a bad attitude can bring down an entire office. Likewise, one that has a hard time meeting your expectations can also hurt the overall success of your office. Hiring the right people is critical. Thus, you should be extremely selective when hiring your next employee. Haste in hiring people backfires in a multitude of ways. It is very expensive to hire, train and motivate employees. This cost multiplies when you look at lost production opportunities and the time consuming process of termination.

Pay as little as you can up front, and if they are great employees, give them bonuses so they never leave. If you pay too much up front, your bad employee will stay forever. After I have narrowed the list of prospective employees and found the one I want to hire, I ask him/her, "I like what you had to say and would like to offer you the position. However, I think you are going to be more expensive than I can afford at this time. If I were to offer you the position, what would you like to earn?" Regardless of their answer, I inform them that was what I expected, and it is too much. I then ask, "What is the minimum that you would have to receive to accept this position today?" I am usually shocked at how little some people say they need. "That's great! What would you think if I developed a pay structure that guarantees you will make $ (the minimum), but if you do a great job, I will offer you bonuses that will allow you to make the income you want to earn?" They can't say no. Now, you have a great compensation program that motivates them to achieve a good result!

Create a Game Your Employees Want to Play

Creating a pay structure which motivates your employees to focus on results-based activities is a critical step in the development of your organizational strategy. Paying a set salary for an employee without an incentive to perform at a higher level will ultimately lead to a bored and frustrated employee. In addition, if you only pay a salary without benefits, your employees will leave you as soon as they find a comparable job with a higher pay structure (See the Employee Handbook in Appendix F).

Be creative when setting an employee's salary. Each employee should have a written agreement which clearly identifies his/ her responsibilities, pay structure, and minimum expectations (See Appendices B–E for Employee Agreements). In my opinion, each employee should have 20–40 percent of his monthly salary subject to a performance-based pay scale. Any more and employees will leave if you set their goals too high. Any less and your employees will not be motivated to focus on income producing activities. Be creative. Every employee can be on a performance-based pay plan. Here are bonuses I have found to be effective:

Pay Structure

- **Operations Manager:** Pay a monthly bonus for each policy growth in the agency.

- **Sales Manager:** Pay your licensed sales manager a percent of the new business commissions written for the entire agency.

- **Retention Specialist**: Pay a monthly bonus for accounts saved and improved retention ratios.

- **Agency Contact Manager:** Pay for every scheduled appointment that comes into the office for an annual policy review.

- **Customer Service Representative:** Pay a monthly bonus for each policy growth in the agency. Pay additional bonuses for cross-sold households.

- **Agency Sales Representative:** Pay commissions with a small base pay.

- **Administrative Assistant:** Even your entry level position can be subject to performance standards. Your admin clerk can be paid for appointments scheduled, updated address/phone cards, and referrals obtained using your agency's emergency contact program.

All Employees

- **Health Insurance:** Offer a health plan to all employees. Even if you do not contribute one hundred percent of the benefits up front, some sort of employer-sponsored plan is a must.

- **Holiday Bonus:** Pay $1 to each employee for each annual policy-in-force gained. To pay this bonus in December, you must use November to November figures.

- **Five Years With Your Agency:** Give extra days of vacation and a choice of maid service, yard service or a health club membership. Each of these benefits will cost you around $150 per month. If you give your employees $150, they remember it for one pay period, maybe two. If you give yard or maid service, your employee will appreciate it for years to come.

- **Spot Bonus:** Encourage creativity every day! When an employee creates a new program or goes over and above what is expected of them, pay a bonus on the spot for everyone to see. The bonus doesn't have to be large. The gesture and gratitude will encourage excitement and motivate them to consistently look for new ways of doing things.

When your employees are compensated for their success, they come to work eager and motivated. In addition, you will never have to increase your employee's base pay again. If they want a raise, they know how to get one: They have to earn it!

The Interview

Never let prospects know that you are interested in making an offer during the first meeting. Inform candidates that the selection process is very competitive, and you will get back in touch if they are selected.

Being able to spot talent in minutes and knowing when to end an interview is crucial to your overall recruiting success. When a candidate comes in for the interview, I like to immediately ask them a simple question, "How are you doing today?" If the candidate starts to complain, that's your cue to ask the next question, "So which position were you coming in to interview for?" And when they respond simply apologize for any inconvenience for failing to contact them when the position was filled late yesterday! "But we will keep you in mind if the position opens again in the future."

As a business owner, you must make certain that you are not only asking effective interview questions, you must avoid asking illegal questions before a conditional offer of employment is made. Focus on relevant qualifications required on the job.

You may ask prospective employees for their name, address, and social security number. Questions about a candidate's age must be limited to whether he or she is eighteen years of age or older; not how old he or she actually is.

You are allowed to inquire whether a candidate is prevented from lawfully becoming employed in this country because of visa or immigration status, and you are also required to document legal residency status.

Other routine **legal** questions are:

- The nature of employment or specific job desired (position, start date, salary sought)
- The name of the candidate's present employer and whether you may contact the applicant's present employer
- Education
- Military service
- Former employers (name, address, salary, position, reason for leaving)
- References
- Emergency contact information

Examples of **illegal** questions are:

- What is your age or date of birth?

- What is your sexual orientation?

- What church do you attend?

- What is your national origin?

- What is your maiden name?

- What is your marital status (Circle one: Ms., Mrs., or Miss)?

- Are you widowed, divorced, or separated?

- What is or was your spouse's name and/or job?

- Have you ever filed a workers' compensation claim?

- Do you have any physical impairments or disabilities that would prevent you from performing the job for which you are applying?

- Have you ever been hospitalized? If so, for what condition?

- Have you ever been treated by a psychiatrist or psychologist? If so, for what condition?

- Is there any health-related reason that you may not be able to perform the job for which you are applying?

- How many days were you absent from work because of illness last year?

- Are you taking any prescribed drugs?

- Have you ever been treated for drug addiction or alcoholism?

If you use an online profile as a pre-selection tool, several companies will give you an effective interview guide which will make certain your questions are within the law. For more information on effective interviewing practices, forms and human resources documents, visit JeffHastingsAgency. com.

Here are a few powerful open-ended interview questions that I have found to be useful. Use them to look for red flags and to determine if your candidate meets your profile.

Ten Powerful Interview Questions

No	Question
1.	Can you tell me a little about yourself and why you have chosen to interview for this position?
2.	As I'm reviewing your resume, I would like to ask you a few questions about the positions you held, the reason you left and what your boss would say if I called him or her to let them know you were applying for this position.
3.	How often have you come in early or worked late to get the job done?
4.	Describe a situation where you created an idea or product that created revenue for a company you have worked for.
5.	Tell me what you like and dislike about your most recent position.
6.	Have you ever worked with a difficult customer? How was the customer being difficult? How did you handle the situation?
7.	Have you ever worked in a commission-based position or where you had to perform to be compensated?
8.	Tell me about some of your accomplishments that you are most proud of.
9.	Where to you see yourself in five years? If you could do anything, what would you do professionally?

No	Question
10.	If you are hired, you would be required to bring in more revenue than you are compensated. Knowing what you know now about the position in which you are applying for, how would you bring revenue into my Agency?

John G. Miller's book, *The Question Behind the Question*, discusses a method of practicing personal accountability. In my opinion, when interviewing, you should look for the answer behind the answer. Here are some red flags:

- If candidates don't like their current position or boss, they will probably not like you as well.

- See how committed your candidates were in their last position. If they seem to have jumped around, this should be a huge red flag.

- Does their family support their decision to enter this field? I have seen quite a few candidates who had exceptional promise fail because they did not have a supportive environment at home.

- Your candidate should have several accomplishments of which they are proud. Get them to open up and brag about their work activities. If they can't think of any, they may be the type of person that just likes to "show up" at work. You need a person who can become a profit center, not a drain on your income.

- Try and determine if your candidate is a self-starter, or if they need to be constantly supervised and told what to do. You are going to be extremely busy running your business. You don't have the time to babysit, and you need to find people who are going to make things happen.

The only way you can find out if candidates are motivated or if they have a burning desire to succeed is by asking questions and listening carefully to their responses. During a first interview, the candidate should be the one speaking most of the time, not you.

I wish I could say that I have the magic answer as to what characteristics make a successful employee, but I don't. I can tell you that my best employees were referrals who had some experience in our industry. All of my top performers are competitive, passionate individuals who dream of having a better life. Most of them are from middle to lower middle class families. They know the value of a hard day's work and are willing to invest the blood, sweat and tears to one day have a better life.

Hiring Office Managers

I'm a big fan of delegation and have hired several office managers. Finding the right manager who looks out for your best interest and not their own is critical to your success. Just because a prospect meets your minimum entry level qualifications, does not mean that you have to offer him the position. To ensure your long term success, you must truly interview candidates and only accept those who have the highest likelihood of success. Because it is very expensive to train one person, it is imperative that you look for quality rather than quantity.

Why Employees Leave

The secret to long-term employee performance is creating an atmosphere that meets the needs of your employees. In today's work environment, it is a must to not only offer health insurance and a financial benefit package; you must create flexible work hours, opportunities for advancement, an emotionally stimulating environment and a clear vision as to where the company is headed.

Profiles International conducted a survey and found the following top five reasons employees leave their employers:[7]

- Boredom

- Inadequate salary and benefits

- Limited opportunities for advancement

- No recognition

- Unhappy with management and the way they were being managed

The study found that of the job-leavers surveyed:

- 30% Were unhappy with management and the way they were managed

- 25% Felt they never received recognition for good work

- 20% Complained of limited opportunities for advancement

---

7   Bud Haney, Jim Sirbasku and Deiric McCann, *40 Strategies for Winning in Business,* (Waco: Profiles International, Inc. 2004), 14.

- 15% Cited inadequate salary and benefits (low, isn't it?)

- 5% Were bored with their job assignments

- 5% Cited other reasons (retirement, career change, sabbatical, and travel)

Develop Your Winning Team

A good man likes a hard boss. I don't mean a nagging boss or a grouchy boss. I mean a boss who insists on things being done right and on time; a boss who is watching things closely enough so that he knows a good job from a poor one. Nothing is more discouraging to a good man than a boss who is not on the job, and who does not know whether things are going well or badly.

— William Feather

Creating a winning environment is essential when you are trying to develop a culture for success. This requires knowledge, leadership and a strong work ethic to help sales reps attain their highest potential. Building a winning team starts the moment the prospective employee comes in for an interview.

Leadership and Self-Awareness

As the owner of a small business, you have taken on an entire new responsibility that you may not be aware of. In fact, there are a multitude of responsibilities unique to a business owner that employees seldom recognize.

First and foremost, you made a commitment to yourself. You *have*, or in some cases *had* a dream of one day taking control of your own future and doing something more with your life. You conducted research, spoke with your loved ones and made the leap knowing that odds were stacked against you.

Next, you made a commitment to your loved ones. The ones who count on you to provide food, clothing and shelter. The ones who count on you to be there when you need them the most. This commitment for most is the driving force behind the long hours and sacrifices you make to realize your dream.

Third, you made or will make a commitment to your employees. Employees who will, in time, seem more like family than merely a name in the office with a job to do. Hire the right ones who will share your dream and buy into your vision and you will feel the weight of this commitment and the unexpected responsibility that comes along with it.

You also have a commitment to your customers who count on you to care about them, understand their needs, recommend the right product and deliver on your promise to be there when they have a claim. This becomes extremely clear if you offer life insurance, and as you progress in your agency witness clients/friends pass without this extremely important protection.

Finally, you have a commitment to the company or companies who gave you this tremendous opportunity. Never get too big to forget how you started. Hundreds of thousands of agents have paved the way for you to take advantage of this incredible opportunity that is in front of you today.

It is my opinion that leaders are made, not born. If you don't consider yourself a good leader, it is never too late to learn. In order to do this, you have to want to work on yourself as a person, to know yourself inside and out and to never stop developing yourself to be the leader that you know is inside of you.

What kind of impact do you think you have on others now? Does your impact match the results that you would like to have? If you are not certain, ask for feedback from those around you. Your friends, family, coworkers and/or a few employees may be a good place to start. Let them know that you are working on self-improvement and you value their opinion. Make them feel safe and don't try and justify your actions or get defensive when they give you their opinion. Hearing feedback like this can be hard to take in and you may experience feelings of insult, hurt or even anger. Resist your temptation to over react and take it all in. Look for common observations and consider what people tell you as objective information you can use to be a better leader.

We have all heard that while we may not be able to have control over what happens to us, we can control our reaction to it. Our past experiences play a significant role of who we are and how we react to others on a daily basis. I never truly understood this until a few years ago when a friend of mine, who is a clinical therapist, made the observation that he believed I worked so hard because of my fear of failure. He knew when I was young, I witnessed my mother go through extremely difficult financial times after her and my fathers divorce. I was a teenager when it happened and can remember having to drop my mother's car off at the car dealership and run because she could no longer afford the car payment. I remember thinking to myself, "I will never let this happen to me!"

Self-awareness gives you the understanding of where you are today, in a realistic point of view that can provide the insight to lead your team to greatness. And to lead your team, you must be aware on how your decisions and attitudes impact others around you. From the way you communicate your message, to the way you listen and respond to their words, your influence can impact others perception of you are, and also the actions of those who follow.

When you start to realize the importance of having an accurate view of who you are combined with an understanding of why you react the way you do, it is then and only then that you can grow into a leader that others want to follow and begin to live a rich and fulfilling life. And when you feel comfortable with this process, share your experiences of self-awareness with others. Don't be afraid to admit your faults and be a role model for others to follow. Tell them how becoming more aware of who you are has positively impacted your life and encourage them to do the same. Tell them how you did it and mentor them through the process.

Leadership is not about standing on a podium and getting others to do what you want them to do. Leadership is about leading yourself and taking complete responsibility for your life. It's about admitting your strengths and weaknesses and not being afraid to ask for help. It's about living with passion, purpose and integrity at all times. It's about doing the right thing even when no one else is watching and setting an example to make this world a better place for just one person or millions. And that's why anyone can become a leader if they are courageous enough to try.

It All Begins With Expectations

So much of what we do and the success we achieve depend upon the expectations we set and consequences imposed. I am not suggesting that you motivate by fear and intimidation. I am merely saying that your staff should clearly understand what is expected of them. Growth should be a minimum expectation, and there should be consequences for their performance.

One winter, a very successful agent, David Sewell, and I took a trip to Chicago to visit with a few highly successful agents. If you have heard David speak, then you know he is a very energetic and passionate guy who has developed one of the most successful insurance agencies in the country. Upon arrival, we decided to grab a bite to eat before calling it a night. David insisted on making one call to the office, and I offered to bring the car around to the front of the hotel. After twenty minutes of waiting, I got impatient enough to find out what was taking so long. I walked in on David having a rather heated discussion with one of his staff members. I heard David say, "Nancy, I was very clear on what I needed you to get done before I left. You have to contact…" he went on for some time making certain his message was clear. He continued, "And I know you have a lot planned for this weekend, but you know how important it is that we get it done! Okay, I've got to go now, someone is waiting on me. I love you, too!" I was shocked to find out that Nancy was his mother-in-law! I couldn't believe what I had just heard. David said Nancy was his office manager, and she knew that during the day they had a job to do. He was very clear about this when he hired her. After hours, she went back to being his mother-in-law.

One month later, I hired my brother Brian. He worked for me for 9-years. My sister Laura also has worked with me for more than 10 years. We have successfully separated work from our personal lives and love working together. The moral of the story is: Family members can be a great and trusted asset on your team, if you manage expectations. If you consider hiring family members or close friends, make certain they clearly understand up front that business is business, and you can go back to being family and friends after hours.

Tracking Employee Performance

As a business owner, you must keep your team focused on working on the activities which are going to positively impact your bottom line. But how do you really know when your employees are making you money, or costing you? While personal observations and a feel for your business are necessary, your observation may not give you the information you need to answer the question.

There is a little known program out there that I've been using to help motivate my employees and to make certain they are focused on the important daily activities that are necessary for me to accomplish my goals.

The program called PODs (www.ipspods.com) was created by a very successful insurance agent in as a solution to better manage employee performance. Using Stephen Covey's theory of time management and the four quadrants of daily activities, the program allows you to first set an income goal, identify what activities need to take place in order to reach that goal and assign each goal to yourself and/or staff members. As you and your staff progress throughout the day, you will keep focused on important activities and check them off as you work.

Results are tracked in real time and can be viewed on computer or any mobile device. Historical trends on quoting activity, close ratio's and such are retained to help you identify what's working and what's not in your agency. You can also use this program to run staff promotions to reward successful performance. When my agents signed up, they gave me a promo code PODsJH and gave us $100 off of the set-up fee. I'm sure they will do the same for you.

Using the PODs program combined with a Quarterly Performance Review will give you a systematic way to quantify employee productivity (see Appendix K).

Breed Healthy Competition

One of the most effective and cheapest motivators for performance that I have ever found is the use of a simple production chart which shows the ranking of each employee. Posting this chart for all to see motivates your staff because they see how they rank against their peers.

If you are a captive agent or work for a general agency, you can also chart your agency's performance against other agencies in your local area. Team up with other agents. Develop a promotion that gets the competitive spirit going in your agency.

Always promote to your staff's needs. Make your staff feel special and create great memories while building your high performance team.

The biggest mistake you could make is to have a promotion and fail to deliver the reward in the end. Never make promises you cannot keep. Your staff will remember for many years small things like dinners that were promised and not delivered.

Paying Commissions to Staff

In college, I was taught that money was not a motivator of behavior. Looking back, I have to believe that the person who made that remark must have had a lot of it! At one point in my life, Ramen noodles were a luxury and money was indeed a motivator. It is true that after reaching the point where you can afford everything you *need* and have some of the items you *want*, money is less of a motivator.

I am a huge believer that you should compensate your staff for performance. In our business, if you don't sell, you don't eat. Everyone on your team should be motivated to sell and compensated accordingly. Before paying your staff for their sales performance, first make sure you are not breaking any insurance laws in the process.

The most important law you should be concerned about is paying commissions to an unlicensed staff member. If you want to pay an unlicensed staff person for sales performance, check with your specific State Department of Insurance to clarify the requirements. Every state has rules concerning the payment of commissions to unlicensed individuals. In Texas, SB414 was enacted in 2003 which allows agents to pay an unlicensed person referral fees...

"as long as the unlicensed person does not act as the agent and does not discuss specific insurance policy terms or conditions with the customer or potential customer. A referral fee may be paid to

such an unlicensed person if the payment is not based upon the purchase of insurance by the customer."

It is a good business practice to get your entire staff properly licensed. The licensing process will give them the education they need to make a good product recommendation and will keep you out of trouble if they start to quote or accept payments for insurance.

My office routinely assists in the training of agent employees. On many occasions, I hear staff members complaining because they do not feel adequately compensated for their performance. Agents often ask me how much commission to pay their staff. My answer is to pay enough to motivate your staff without going broke in the process.

Here is an easy way to calculate how much you should pay your staff. First, let's assume your employee needs to earn at least $2,000 per month, but would like to earn more. This employee is a Customer Service Representative, and you expect her to cross-sell at every opportunity. Your minimum expectation is for her to bring in at least ten new accounts (five automobile policies and five homeowners policies) per month. Your average annual commission on homeowners policies is $150 and auto is $100 per vehicle. If you expect your employee to bring in at least $500 in new auto commissions ($100 x 5 = $500) and $750 in new homeowners commissions ($150 x 5 = $750), you should give your licensed employee a base of $1,500 and a 50% commission on new business. This would give her $2,125 (1,500 + 250 + 375) in monthly income for selling ten policies.

The good news is that if she does not sell any policies during the month, she will barely pay the bills. If she doubles her sales efforts, she will earn $2,750 (1,500 + 500 + 750) per month. "Wait a second!" you may say, "I can't afford $2,750 per month." But can you? Remember, if she sells twenty policies per month, she will make $2,500 in commissions for you. She will service your entire business and 85 percent of the customers will renew their policies in twelve months. This employee is a bargain!

We have all heard the saying, "You get what you pay for." When it comes to hiring employees, this is dead on! There is a significant difference between a $1,500 per month employee and a $3,000 per month one. Don't be afraid to spend money on quality people. If you do it right, a great employee is the best business investment you can ever make!

Hold Weekly Staff Meetings

It is surprising to me how many business owners fail to have regular staff meetings with their team. Whether you have one employee or fifteen, you must hold meetings at least once per week to identify problems and to keep your employees focused on important activities. Be prepared to discuss the prior week's accomplishments and failures. Share your vision with your staff often and hold them accountable for their performance.

Increase the Effectiveness of Your Staff Meetings

How often have you conducted (or sat through) a staff meeting by spending 3–4 hours going over stacks of information in hopes that a few employees will leave motivated to make the changes necessary to help you meet your goals? The truth is although most meetings may be good enough to pass along information, they rarely motivate employees to change their behavior, and results will stay the same.

Who can blame us? Most of us have never been trained on how to hold an effective staff meeting. In addition, there is no substitute for the value of face-to-face meetings. In this fast-paced world that we live in, time is extremely valuable, and we simply don't have the time to meet with each team member as often as we would like.

After attending a workshop in my company's training facility, I realized that my meetings had to change. First of all, I needed to create a safe learning environment that encourages the participants to come up with solutions to the problems at hand. To hold an effective meeting, I made the following changes that significantly improved the success of my staff meetings and training programs:

- Always start meetings on a positive note. Spend a few minutes discussing how everyone is doing and take a few minutes to talk about non-work issues.

- Acknowledge success and give praise when praise is warranted. Ask your employee to talk about how they came up with an idea or implemented a program that is improving the success of the office.

- When you have extremely important information to discuss, send out an agenda before the meeting to generate interest about the topics to be addressed.

- Schedule meetings before lunch.

- Start the meeting on time — every time.

- Keep the participants on track and focused.

- Have a structured reporting format for each employee to discuss the prior week's results and the priorities to accomplish in the current week.

- Do not tell participants they are wrong or humiliate them in front of their peers.

- Encourage creativity. Face it, you do not know all of the answers!

- From time to time, ask for feedback when the meeting is over. Look for ways to make the next meeting even better.

Organize a Staff Retreat

An annual staff retreat away from the office will help you steer your team in the right direction. It doesn't have to be in a fancy hotel or resort. Sometimes, we simply meet at a country club or local restaurant. Other times, we take my boat out and spend the day brainstorming about ways we can improve our life insurance sales performance.

Hire a phone service or leave a detailed message on your office phone letting your customers know that you are closing the office for the day to brainstorm new, innovative ways to improve your agency's performance. In case of emergencies, leave your cell phone number for assistance. Your customers will appreciate your efforts if your message is clear that you are doing your best to improve the service provided by your agency.

I open the meeting by presenting the "State of the Agency" address. During my opening, I discuss the prior year's goals, successes and failures. After my review, I discuss the next year's goals and objectives and the new roles of every staff member. Everything is neatly organized and printed, so each employee can easily follow along without any mixed messages.

Staff members take turns giving presentations on their accomplishments and failures in the current year. In addition, they share what they will do in the upcoming year to improve results. It is also important to address any problems that may hinder employee productivity.

If you find yourself failing to meet your production goals, it may be necessary to meet away from the office more than once per year. The most important thing is to get every team member focused on setting goals and being accountable for their own actions. In addition, it gives them a clear understanding of your vision for the future of your agency operation and what is expected of them.

As an agency owner, you must add value to your employee's performance. You have a responsibility to help your team achieve their maximum potential. If you fail to pay attention to them and give them the tools they need to be successful, your employees will lose interest in your business and will take advantage of the unsupervised time in your office.

Develop Strong Personal Relationships With Your Employees

I have read numerous books on why you should not have close relationships with people who report to you. I disagree. To effectively run a team, you must develop strong personal relationships with your staff. The personal relationships build a family spirit within your organization. I can't tell you the number of times I have been the first person my employees called to announce the birth of a child or when they just needed someone to listen to them. I'm honored to be that person. I celebrate their achievements with them, and when they fail, I feel that a part of me has failed as well.

I can sincerely say that I love many of my employees and would do anything for them. I don't usually shake hands with someone I care about. I hug. These strong personal relationships keep me going when times get tough and allow me to go to my team when I need them most. Without this emotional connection, there is no good reason for your employees to risk doing whatever it takes to help you become successful.

Think about it: Why do your employees love to get up and come into the office each morning? Why do they love being part of your team? What motivates them to work for a common cause? If you can answer these questions with little effort, you're doing a great job! If not, you may want to find a way to express your love for your work and the people who help build your business.

Technology

In today's market, it is imperative that you have a laptop computer or iPad and a smart phone with a hot spot, which gives you Internet access from anywhere in your operating territory. Get a high-end computer that will last you a few years with a large hard drive, dual monitors and plenty of memory to run the latest software. Even if you have just a single employee, I also recommend you have a dedicated server which will keep your office running smoothly while also giving you a place to back up your files daily.

Back up your data! I'm shocked at how many small business owners have years of hard work saved on their computers and fail to have their data saved on another computer. It's not a matter of *if* your computer crashes, it's a matter of *when*.

I like to walk into an agent's office and say, "You came into the office this morning and found that someone had broken into your office and stolen your computers. How would your business suffer?" Yes, some of my agents look at me as if I am crazy, but they get the point. It's not good enough to simply have a server. The server can be taken from your office too. Here are my recommendations to help make certain you have the proper data recovery program in place at all times:

- Have a dedicated server and give every employee space on the hard drive to back up their data files. Employees should back-up their data every Friday before they leave the office.

- Make sure your personal computer has mirrored RAID hard drives. When one drive fails, the other drive continues without hesitation or loss of data.

- Take it from someone who has been broken into three times. Purchase a very large external hard drive and attach it to your computer. Bolt this hard drive to the back of a large piece of furniture out of sight. When your office is broken into, the thieves will quickly take all new PCs and monitors. The cords will be left on your desk. These guys are in a hurry, they are not going to bother with disconnecting everything and taking the cords. Use this hard drive to automatically back-up your server data nightly.

- Use a "cloud-based" service like Dropbox.com to automatically sync your critical work data with your home computer. Programs like Dropbox allow you to have a secure data back-up plan in place, have access to your files anywhere in the world via smart phone and iPad, and share files with your employees and work on projects simultaneously.

- Use the latest anti-virus software, and update it daily!

- Make certain your employees are informed that computers are for business use only. Do not allow employees to download unauthorized files, especially music. It doesn't matter if they are on their lunch hour or not, music downloads slow down your entire network and open up your computer system for extremely damaging viruses. Have your employees sign a document annually acknowledging this understanding and inform them not to use instant messaging or other personal emails from their business account. Everything they do on their work PC can be monitored by your network administrator. I could write another book on decreased workforce productivity due to instant messaging, Facebook, and personal emails, but I don't have the time. All I can tell you is that although you don't want to make your employees feel uncomfortable or believe they have no privacy, you must do your best to keep your employees focused on income producing activities.

- Purchase surveillance cameras and install them in very visible locations throughout your office. I haven't had a break-in since installing cameras.

Create a Family Atmosphere

Create a family atmosphere within your company. Have an annual agency picnic. Invite all employees, families and customers to come. Give every child a gift. Get your employees together as often as possible to converse outside of their normal working environment. Build true friendships with them, and show them how much you appreciate their efforts.

Part IX

Balance Is the Key to Long-Term Success

It isn't success if it costs you the companionship and chumminess and love of your children. Very often, busy, wealthy men of momentous affairs discover too late that they have sacrificed the finest thing in life, the affection of their family.

— B. C. Forbes

He who dies with the most toys is still dead. If there is any part of this book that you should read twice, it's this chapter.

The most successful business owners take time to relax and enjoy the fruits of their labor. Owning a business can be extremely stressful and failure to relax can cause tension, mental exhaustion, and poor health. Your business should *give* you more life; it should not *be* your life.

Success means different things to different people, and my definition is different today than it was a few short years ago. Most entrepreneurs relate success to money, until something happens in their lives to change their perception. I'm not against making money and still rank it high on my list of priorities. However, I realize that you can never get time back to spend with your spouse and children. Now that I realize this and have my priorities right, I am happier, healthier and more productive than ever before.

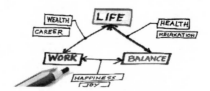

Develop a Balanced Lifestyle

When I first began in this business, I came out of the gate trying to set the world on fire. Nothing was going to stand in my way of becoming one of the elite small business owners in the company. Success to me was defined by money and recognition. My dream was to be named the "District Manager of the Year."

In early 1999, my business was running on all cylinders. My day usually started around 6:00 A.M., and I made it a point to arrive in the office before my employees so that I could plan my schedule according to the important tasks that must be achieved. With so much going on, I seldom made it home in time for dinner. On more times than I would like to admit, I arrived after my family had turned in for the night. I didn't see my family often and my wife eventually gave up caring and quickly found a way to manage on her own. I viewed time at home as a luxury that small business owners could not afford and I was willing to sacrifice almost anything for my own success. Because of my passion and commitment for this success, I rarely slept well on Sunday nights because I was excited about going into the office the next day!

Eventually my health deteriorated and on the morning of October 15, 2000, my body had all that it could handle. Mentally and physically fatigued, I sat at my computer feeling light-headed and barely able to hold a cup of coffee. It took all I had to get in my car and drive to my doctor's office. My doctor immediately sent me to the emergency room where they determined that I was severely dehydrated. Although it took a few more years to correctly diagnose an underlying medical condition, it was very clear even then that the stress was taking its toll on my body, and I had to find another way.

For most people, a few emergency room visits, two colonoscopies and an endoscope would be enough for them to get the hint to slow down and take care of their health. Not me. I wanted to be the best and continued to work non-stop. Four years later, with my health continuing to be questionable, my wife and I discovered we had grown too far apart and seemed to be more like roommates than partners. In the heat of an argument, she said something that I will never forget: "One day, you may be District Manager of the Year, but just remember that you lost your entire family because of it!" We separated and were divorced shortly thereafter.

In September 2005, when they called me up to the podium to accept the award, I could barely hold back the tears. Although I was extremely honored and proud to accept this award, as I walked up to the stage, the overwhelming emotions that I had held back for so long, the years of hard work and sacrifice, all came down to this moment that seemed to be frozen in time. Then and only then did I realize that I had given up a part of my life that I would never get back.

Nevertheless, I realize now that maintaining a balanced lifestyle is healthy for me, good for my family and great for my business. I truly believe that I would have the same results, if not better, had I learned to relax, spend quality time with my family and take the time to enjoy life.

I have to admit that this chapter has been the most difficult to write. It's never easy discussing your mistakes, much less writing about them for others to read. Yet, if I save one person from making the same mistakes, it is worth my embarrassment.

Eat Healthy and Keep Physically Fit

Do you get tired during a normal workday? After a hard day's work, do you feel as if it takes all you have just to stay awake on your commute home?

I can tell you first hand that you will become more productive, have a clearer mind and will sleep better if you eat the right things and spend at least 30–45 minutes a day doing some type of exercise. It is a fact that feeling good about yourself will give you more energy, keep you motivated and will help you keep a positive mental attitude.

If your breakfast consists of six cups of coffee before noon, your body may become addicted to caffeine which can lead to hypertension and countless other negative side effects. Try to get at least 7–8 hours of uninterrupted sleep. Rise early and eat a health breakfast. Limit your caffeine intake and eat healthy snacks throughout the day. Your day should not consist of eating lunch at your desk or while working on your computer. Get out of the office and take a real lunch break, which will re-energize you and clear your mind.

Instead of placing candy jars throughout the office, bring grapes and other fruit to satisfy your hunger. Instead of watching the news late at night before you call it a day, take a nice relaxing hot bath before you hit the sack. In just two weeks, you will feel and look like a new person.

If I haven't given you enough reasons to eat right and exercise, here are a few more:

- Limiting caffeine and eating healthy will make you sleep better.
- Getting a full night's rest will reduce the bags under your eyes.
- Getting a full night's rest will give you more energy.
- Having more energy will make you more productive in the office.
- Having more energy will make it easier for you to go to the gym and exercise.
- Exercise will relieve stress and anxiety.

- Exercise relieves digestive disorders and improves your health.

- Exercise enhances your self-image.

- Improving your self-image will increase your chance of having an active sex life.

- Eating right, exercising and having an active sex life will help you live longer.

- Living longer will allow you to enjoy all of the money you earn after developing a successful insurance agency!

Relax

Make an appointment with yourself and take some time every day to relax. Even if it is just for thirty minutes, make some quiet time to recharge your batteries and meditate. I have to admit that this is one piece of advice I need to take myself.

I love to sit in a relaxing chair, listen to classical music and read a good book. Find out what helps you relax and put it on your calendar every day. Give yourself permission to relax.

PART X

Where Do We Go From Here?

If you have nothing else to do, look about you and see if there isn't something close at hand that you can improve! It may make you wealthy, though it is more likely that it will make you happy.

— George Matthew Adams

So, where do you go from here? I sincerely hope that I have given you enough pros and cons to make an informed decision about entering this fast-paced, rapidly changing, and potentially highly rewarding career.

At this point, if this career is right for you, you should be more excited now than ever before about becoming a self-employed agent. If you are greatly concerned about the hard work and lack of guarantees this career provides, I strongly recommend that you conduct further research before leaping into the world of self-employment. This is not a decision that should be made half-heartedly. If you are to succeed, you have to give 110 percent and have the support of your family as well.

So, what's next? Well, I'm not sure what the answer is for you, but I do know this: If you don't do anything different, nothing is going to change. I recommend that you first determine where you want to be in five years. Once you figure out where you want to be, then and only then can you develop the road map of how to get there. Innovate your vision, develop your plan and execute.

So, we've covered a lot of material! To better sum things up and to truly give you a step-by-step approach to a successful agency, I've developed a list of 100 steps that I've covered throughout this book. It may take you up to two years to complete all of these steps. But if you do, you will be well on your way to a successful insurance agency!

100 Steps to a Successful Insurance Agency

1. Discover your passion and remember your dreams. You only have one life to live and this may be the last career move you will ever make.

2. Define success and what it means to you. Keep in mind that your business should give you more life, not become your life.

3. Determine if owning a business and specifically an insurance agency is right for you and your family.

4. If you have a significant other, discuss this opportunity with them. Will this business help you achieve what it is you both want out of life? Understand that some amount

of sacrifice will have to be made early on while you build your agency.

5. Start an exercise routine, even if it's just a quick 10-minute morning walk with your spouse in the morning. Your old routine is gone and you will now start to develop new habits. The key here is to develop healthy habits and maintain a balanced lifestyle. If exercising is new to you, don't do this every other day—do it daily! No excuses, no days off. Don't give yourself an opportunity to procrastinate healthy habits.

6. Conduct your research and seek the opinions and support of your family and friends. Find out what they like and dislike about their current insurance agent.

7. Identify your niche market.

8. Interview with several companies before making your selection. Make certain your niche market is in align with your chosen carrier.

9. After determining which channel and Company to represent, find a mentor that you feel will support you throughout your career.

10. Create your vision for success. Your vision should become crystal clear in your mind and you should be able to answer the question of what makes you different from the competition and why your prospects should buy from you.

11. Write down and share your vision with your loved ones.

12. Review your time management system. Time is your most precious asset. Use it wisely.

13. Find out which licenses you will need for your chosen path. Immediately start studying for your exams.

14. Read the EMyth Revisited by Michael Gerber to find out why most small businesses fail and what to do about it. If married, get your spouse involved and have him read the book as well.

15. Sign-up for the EMyth on-line web portal and start to work "on" your business instead of just "in" it. Allow EMyth to help you create the foundation of a successful business even before you sell your first policy.

16. Complete "Values, Passion and Purpose" on your EMyth web portal.

17. Interview successful agents and find out what they did to become so successful. Document your findings for future reference.

18. Interview unsuccessful agents and avoid the same mistakes. Document your findings for future reference.

19. Pass your insurance licensing exams.

20. Celebrate with your family! Never lose sight of what you are working for.

21. Complete "Connecting with your Customer" on your EMyth web portal.

22. Start product training with your new mentor.

23. Complete "Brand Based Recruiting" on your EMyth web portal.

24. Develop your organizational chart to help clarify and explain your vision to others.

25. Create a template which will be used to create Employee Agreements for every position identified above. Templates can be found on JeffHastingsAgency.com.

26. Start your Agency Development Guide (ADG) which will document every system used in your office and update it frequently.

27. Create a template for your Employee Handbook. A template can be found at JeffHastingsAgency.com.

28. Seek the advice of your mentor to help you complete an Employee Agreement for a Customer Service Representative and a Contact Manager.

29. Complete "Reaching the Right Customer" on your EMyth web portal.

30. File a DBA and open your business accounts under your business name.

31. Apply for a business line of credit.

32. Work with a CPA to set-up your accounts in Quick-Books.

33. Complete "Creating a Cash Plan" and "Building a Budget with Vision" on your EMyth web portal.

34. Identify at least 4 active and 4 passive marketing programs and take the time to write a detailed plan on how each will be used to grow your agency. Update your ADG.

35. Organize your Contact Management System and start to build your database of quality leads. Update your ADG.

36. Complete "Understanding Why They Buy" on your EMyth web portal.

37. If you haven't already done so, schedule a date night once a week with your spouse and stick to it! Opening a business is stressful enough and you can't afford to go through a divorce.

38. Read Tradigital by Angela Johnson and Nadeem Damani.

39. Complete "Developing Your Channels" on your EMyth web portal.

40. Use Facebook to identify prospective leads, LinkedIn to develop business relationships and Twitter to communicate with everyone above.

41. Write down how your agency will use Social Networking to grow your business. Update your ADG.

42. Create a sales system that leaves no stone unturned. From the first contact to closing the sale, you should develop scripts that appeal to your target customer on an emotional level which encourages them to buy your product. Update your ADG.

43. Prepare a professional sales presentation with handouts explaining coverage options and discounts which may be available when customers purchase more than one line of business from your agency. Update your ADG.

44. Practice your scripts in front of your mentor.

45. Create a "10 Reasons to do Business with My Agency" list. Use this list to assist you in your presentation. Print it out and attach it to the front of every sales presentation packet. Update your ADG.

46. Set-up an office with your mentor or get a 6-month lease in an executive suite.

47. Update your Contact Management System to track all quotes to track your competitive position. Salesforce. com is a great tool to accomplish this goal. Update your ADG.

48. Complete "Managing Your Time" on your EMyth web portal. Now that you are licensed and have the basic training to sell insurance, make sure to schedule all business development work in non-sales hours. All bills that need to be paid, org charts, Employee Agreements and such should be worked on before 10 AM and after work. Set time to review your emails before work, once during the day and once before you call it a night. Don't get bogged down behind a computer when you need to be out meeting prospective clients.

49. Issue your first policy.

50. Take a picture with your first client and frame it for your future office wall!

51. Write a "Welcome to Our Agency" letter and send it out to every new client immediately after purchasing their first policy in your agency. Identify staff, background and responsibilities when possible. Update your ADG.

52. Take a picture of the house you live in and the car you currently drive. As you develop a successful small business and start to acquire nicer "things", never forget where you came from.

53. Send your spouse or significant other a gift or flowers at his or her office when you issue your first policy. Let your loved one know how much you appreciate the support and then go out for a nice celebration dinner.

54. Send your mentor a "thank you" card.

55. Develop an effective referral program and write down what works. Update your ADG.

56. Create a contact program which touches your clients in a positive way throughout the year. I use www.cardsby-ana.com which is a Send Out Cards service. If you sign-up using that site, send me an email with your account number and I will send you my card campaigns for free. Update your ADG.

57. Invest in your agency. Make good, sound financial decisions and take advantage of opportunities where your return on your investment is positive.

58. Develop an Interview Questionnaire for future employees.

59. After you feel comfortable with the sales process and have a steady flow of leads coming into your agency, hire a Contact Manager (CM) to answer your phone and set appointments.

60. Set-up payroll with a professional payroll service.

61. Complete "Your Unique Sales Process" on your EMyth web portal.

62. Train your Contact Manager on how to set appointments. Have your Contact Manager document your ADG.

63. Document personal events in your Contact Management System. Do more than the average agent who send birthday cards. Remember wedding anniversaries and other special events to strengthen your relationship with your customers.

64. Don't forget your spouse and family! Remember the date night? It would be horrible to have a program to remember client anniversaries' and not your own!

65. Develop a system to consistently develop relationships with Realtors, loan officers, title companies and others to improve your referral system. Document your ADG.

66. Join a Business Networking International (BNI) chapter in your local community.

67. Find an on-line profile system to help you select future sales producers and employees.

68. When you find yourself missing sales opportunities because you are personally doing CSR work, hire your first CSR.

69. Complete "Your Organizational Roadmap" on your EMyth web portal.

70. Start looking for an office location. Meet with your mentor to determine the best possible location for your new business. Don't make a location decision based on your current home. Make your decision based on the best opportunity for growth for your agency.

71. Get your CSR licensed as soon as possible. Always have at least 1 licensed employee in your office at all times.

72. Meet with your staff weekly to discuss goals and opportunities for growth.

73. Use your Contact Manager to contact customers after being insured with your agency for two years to review product coverage and uncover new opportunities. Write down your script and have your CM update your ADG.

74. Hire a part-time contract Retention Specialist and have her work on programs to make your customers feel special. As she improves her retention systems, have her update the ADG.

75. Recognize your employees for their creativity and betterment of your agency during staff meetings. Share in the wealth. Pay a spot bonus in front of staff when ideas generate revenue for your agency.

76. Promote to your staff on a frequent basis. Create games that employees want to play.

77. Complete "Selling with Integrity" on your EMyth web portal. Insist on the highest ethical standards in everything you do. Document your high standards in your ADG.

78. Contact a professional office leasing agent to review potential office locations. Look for advice from your mentor on how to set-up your office to best support future growth.

79. When you sign a lease, keep in mind that if you do it right, your agency will rapidly grow and so will the need be for additional office space. The longer the lease, the more space you will need. If you cannot afford to take on the amount of space you think you will need, sublease space to a loan processor or Realtor who will give you referrals.

80. Complete "Creating Your Look and Feel" on your EMyth web portal.

81. Have an open house.

82. Look for Trade Shows and community events to start advertising your agency.

83. Organize a staff retreat and keep your employees informed of growth opportunities. Set expectations and continue to recognize and reward exceptional performance.

84. Create a culture of success where employees are excited to come to work.

85. Complete "An Experience Worth Talking About" on your EMyth web portal.

86. Invest in technology. All employees should have dual monitors and smart phones to receive business email on their phones. Reimburse employees for data use when necessary.

87. Improve your cross-sales system. Document your ADG.

88. Improve your staff training program.

89. Complete "Systemizing Excellence" on your EMyth web portal.

90. Require your licensed employees to memorize a sales script and rehearse until perfected.

91. Survey current clients to see how you can improve the performance of your agency. Surveymonkey.com is a free service that will assist you in this process. For a small fee, the site will allow you to save survey results and build a data base to track improvement.

92. Create a Business Exit Interview to find out why customers leave you. An example can be found at JeffHastingsAgency.com. Update your ADG.

93. Complete "Developing Great People" on your EMyth web portal.

94. Conduct Quarterly Employee Performance Reviews.

95. Measure your results and report successes and areas needing improvement to staff.

96. Complete "Tracking Your Progress" on your EMyth web portal.

97. Give back to the community.

98. Give thanks.

99. Take time to relax and enjoy all life has to offer.

100.   Carpe Diem—Seize the Day!

Make Something Happen

I hope the time we have spent together has been beneficial, and you picked up a few ideas. If there is any additional advice I can give you, it would be to make something happen every day that will positively impact the results of your business. Don't leave the office until you've made that one contact, gotten that referral or started that one fire.

As business owners, we have much for which to be thankful. Even during the worst of times, our lives are pretty good. Thank God for the life that He has blessed you with, and make the most of every opportunity. The American Dream is yours for the taking!

Good luck and God bless you,

Tools to Assist You in Management

APPENDIX A - PERSONALITY ASSESSMENT

Circle your answer for each question. Write your score in the score column and add your total.

Ratings:

- SA- Strongly Agree
- A-Agree
- N-Neutral
- D-Disagree
- SD-Strongly Disagree

Statement	SA	A	N	D	SD	Score
1. I have to finish all work before leaving the office for the day.	10	8	6	4	2	
2. Oftentimes, small details distract me from the big picture.	1	2	3	4	5	
3. I have a difficult time delegating work because I believe I would do a better job than anyone else.	1	2	3	4	5	
4. I prefer a commission-only position with high earning potential as opposed to a salary-based position with an acceptable steady income.	15	12	8	6	3	
5. I am the person to whom my friends and family turn in times of need.	5	4	3	2	1	
6. I effectively identify, analyze and solve problems.	15	12	8	6	3	
7. People who know me say I am comfortable with taking risks.	10	8	6	4	2	
8. The key people in my life support my interests and pursuits.	10	8	6	4	2	
9. I do my best work when under pressure.	5	4	3	2	1	
10. I am a self-motivator.	15	12	8	6	3	
11. I am comfortable speaking in front of large groups.	10	8	6	4	2	
12. I have difficulty handling rejection.	2	4	6	8	10	
13. I often work late to finish a task.	5	4	3	2	1	
14. I often attend social functions.	15	12	8	6	3	
15. I have a positive attitude more often than not.	10	8	6	4	2	
Total						

An explanation of scores is given on the next page.

Understanding Your Score

120 and Above: What are you waiting for? You have the qualities that it takes to become a highly successful small business owner.

110–119: You have potential for entrepreneurial success. Review your answers closely and determine who you need to hire to compensate for a few of your weaknesses. All-in-all, this is a good score.

94–109: Maybe working for yourself is not best for you. If you select this career, find a company that will allow you to retain your current position while you are in training. This will give you a chance to find out first-hand if this is something you will enjoy doing.

93 and Below: You need to seriously consider if this career is right for you and your family. This score does not mean you cannot be successful. It simply means you may need to start out with a company that allows you the security of starting as an employee before becoming an independent contractor.

APPENDIX B - BUSINESS PLAN

[Your Logo Here]

The _____Agency

Street Address

Suite # City, State Zip

Business Plan

Prepared by:

Name Agent/Owner Date

Mission Statement

The mission of the [name of agency] is to be a highly recognized and respected insurance agency in the [city] area, serving our client's total insurance needs through life, health, home, auto and commercial insurance. Our purpose is to develop a reputation as a knowledgeable, professional insurance agency that offers personalized products and services focused on meeting our customers' needs. We take pride in the quality of our products and the quality of our service.

Agency History

The agency was founded by [owner's name] in [year]. Prior to starting [name of agency], [owner's name] was the [give prior position and company]. The agency serves the needs of personal insurance consumers in the [city] and surrounding areas.

Executive Summary

This business plan is designed to meet the five-year objectives of the [name of agency]. In five years, it is my goal to have a fully staffed office with total agency revenue of at least $350,000. The agency will be built upon the principles of providing total solutions to the client's needs and marketing. It is our goal to have 280 households, with an average of three policies per household, in five years.

Marketing Strategy

The city of [city] is located in [location] and currently has a population of approximately [number] people. Our strategy is to target [your detailed market strategy].

In the beginning, substantial resources will be used to market to new accounts. As my policies in force (PIF) increases, emphasis will be placed on selling additional lines and policies to these existing household accounts. Early staffing will include one to two telemarketers as well as a contact manager. Additional staff to be added beginning in the second year includes one customer service representative and at least one agency producer.

Five-Year Goals

The five-year goals of the agency are:
- Annual Revenue: $377,000
- Cumulative PIF: 2,300+
- 280 households with an average of three policies per household.
- Maintain a profitable book of business.
- Participate in continuing education—complete LUTC designation.
- Manage finances to fund growth and meet financial obligations.
- Maintain a retention ratio of at least 92 percent.

Key Year-End Benchmark Goals

Year One: Level I

- Agency Revenue: $67,000
- Cumulative PIF: 334
- Create the vision of what the agency will look like once it is complete.
- Start the business plan and *Agency Employee Handbook.*
- Define our marketing strategy and identify business differentiation.
- Implement at least 2 passive and 6 active marketing programs.
- Staff: I part-time employee

Year Two: Level I

- Agency Revenue: $146,000
- Cumulative PIF: 752
- Open office (This is preferable to being in an office with a Sales Manager during year one).
- Continue to adjust Business Plan and complete Office Employee Guide.
- Master marketing skills and activities.
- Begin Life Underwriters Training Council program (LUTC).
- Continue using at least 3 passive and 5 active marketing programs.
- Staff: I part-time and I full-time employee

Year Three: Level II

- Agency Revenue: $223,000
- Cumulative PIF: 1,213
- Complete LUTC designation.
- Document marketing system.
- Continue using 4 passive and 4 active marketing programs.

- Staff: 2.5 employees and one Outside Sales Rep (Agency Producer)

Year Four: Level III

- Agency Revenue: $310,000
- Cumulative PIF: 1,757
- Staff: 3.5 employees and 2 Agency Producers

Year Five: Level III (with Level IV in sight)

- Agency Revenue: $402,000
- Cumulative PIF: 2,332
- Departmentalize organization. Start grooming your VP of Marketing and VP of Operations.
- Staff: 4.5 employees and 3 Agency Producers

Five Year Organizational Chart

[Include Your Proposed Organizational Chart Here]

Your Five-Year Organizational Chart should reflect the expansion plans for your agency. If you plan to grow and continue meeting the goals and aspirations that you have set for yourself, you cannot continue performing all phases of your operation yourself. You must eventually hire help, and the sooner the better.

Your first employee will probably be a part-time Customer Service Rep. The positions and functions you fill will change over time. A five-year organizational chart will help you plan for such changes. Eventually, you will need staff members to handle office administration, claims, prospecting, contact management, policy reviews and customer service. Use this five-year organizational chart as a road map to guide you through future staffing.

Yearly Goals and Action Plans
Year One Goals

- Agency Revenue: $67,000
- Cumulative PIF: 334

Action Plans

- Complete licensing requirements according to state guidelines.

- Complete corporate training programs.

- Identify a clear vision of what my agency will look like when it is complete.

- Set-up DBA and open commercial bank account with credit line.

- Start using QuickBooks to track business expenses.

- Consult with a CPA to prepare for income tax liability.

- Use a payroll service to handle employee paychecks.

- Identify target markets and create marketing programs.

- Use ACT or another contact management program to track prospects.

- Obtain at least one center of influence per week.

- Hire one part-time Customer Service Rep to handle routine transactions so I can focus on selling.

- Produce at least 17 auto, 8 fire, 1 commercial and 3 life policies each month.

- Sign-Up for the E-Myth web platform by going to: http://bit.ly/emythcoach

Recommended Reading:

- *The E-Myth Revisited* by Michael E. Gerber.
- *Power Position Your Agency* by Troy Korsgaden

Yearly Goals and Action Plans
Year Two Goals

- Agency Revenue: $146,000
- Cumulative PIF: 752

Action Plans

- Find an acceptable office location and move in by the end of the year.
- Begin LUTC program.
- Review state continuing education guidelines to ensure compliance.
- Enhance business plan.
- Complete documentation of my marketing strategy.
- Verify referral programs to ensure they are working as planned.
- Mail birthday, anniversary and holiday cards to all clients.
- Master marketing skills.
- Set up money market and investment accounts to fund future growth and meet income tax obligations.
- Hire an additional full-time staff member who is trained to handle all application processing.
- Produce at least 22 auto, 11 fire, 4 life and 2 commercial polices per month.

Recommended Reading:

- *Profit from Change* by Troy Korsgaden
- *The Norm Levine Reader* by Norman Levine

Yearly Goals and Action Plans
Year Three Goals

- Agency Revenue: $223,000
- Cumulative PIF: 1,213

Action Plans

- Increase advertising budget to include ads in the local newspaper.
- Improve education in commercial-lines insurance.
- Complete documentation of marketing strategy.
- Develop an exit survey to find out why customers leave the agency. Complete LUTC designation.
- Improve life insurance training to handle large cases.
- Develop a relationship with an attorney to handle estate planning for your clients.
- Start an employee-sponsored retirement program.
- Hire an additional full-time employee and one Outside Sales Rep.
- Develop a systematic way to conduct annual policy reviews.
- Focus on new programs to improve policy retention.
- Produce at least 25 auto, 13 fire, 5 life and 2 commercial policies per month.
- Hire a Professional Business Coach. You can hire a certified EMyth Coach by going to:
  coach.emyth.com/jeffhastings

Recommended Reading:

- *The Attitude of Leadership* by Keith Harrell
- *Raving Fans* by Ken Blanchard

Yearly Goals and Action Plans
Year Four Goals

- Agency Revenue: $288,000
- Cumulative PIF: 1,757

Action Plans

- Complete development and documentation of cross- selling systems.
- Develop a program to win back clients who have left the agency.
- Send a survey to review your results through the eyes of your clients.
- Create a quarterly newsletter to inform clients of agency changes and insurance market news.
- Develop a relationship with a respected local Realtor® and share referrals and advertising costs.
- Review state-specific continuing education requirements.
- Hire an additional employee and an Agency Sales Producer.
- Develop a program to follow up on the handling of customer claims.
- Produce at least 30 auto, 15 fire, 6 life and 2 commercial policies monthly.

Recommended Reading:

- *The Greatest Salesman in the World* by Og Mandino
- *The Power of Focus* by Jack Canfield

Yearly Goals and Action Plans
Year Five Goals

- Agency Revenue: $378,000
- Cumulative PIF: 2,332

Action Plans

- Start to departmentalize the business into Marketing, Finance and Operations.
- Make certain all employees understand the agency's vision and are focused on achieving your goals.
- Hire an Agency Contact Manager to contact existing customers, thank them for their business and schedule annual policy reviews with a Sales Rep.
- Meet with a CPA to consider incorporating.
- Review personal retirement program.
- Invest at least 5% of gross revenue in retirement savings.
- Give back to the community by sponsoring local charity events.
- Produce at least 35 auto, 18 fire, 7 life and 3 commercial policies monthly.

Recommended Reading:

- *E-Myth Mastery* by Michael Gerber
- *Good to Great* by Jim Collins

APPENDIX C - CSR
AGREEMENT

**Customer Service Representative
Individual Employment Agreement**

Agent Name, DBA Agent, hereinafter called EMPLOYER, of (address), and **Employee Name**, DBA Customer Service Representative hereinafter called EMPLOYEE, of   intending to be legally bound hereby, agree as follows:

This agreement will take effect on   (month/day), 20 .

EMPLOYER and EMPLOYEE shall be associated as EMPLOYER and EMPLOYEE at the rate of compensation as follows: **EMPLOYER shall pay EMPLOYEE the sum of _____\$ per hour.**

Performance Bonuses

Because the Customer Service Representative will play a key role in the overall success of the Agency, the EMPLOYEE will be compensated for successful performance.

Monthly

Monthly bonuses will be paid on the fifteenth of the month as follows:

- \$2 for every gain in policies-in-force (PIF gain)
- \$25 for every new household/new policy brought into the Agency
- \$10 for every existing household/new policy cross-sell generated by the EMPLOYEE

- $20 for every life appointment set by the EMPLOYEE (appointment must show-up)

Annual

- $1 for every PIF gain in the agency

Medical

In addition, after 90 days of employment, the EMPLOYER agrees to pay one-half of the EMPLOYEE'S monthly medical insurance premiums if the EMPLOYEE participates in the Agency medical insurance program. The EMPLOYEE will pay one-half of his/her medical insurance premiums and the entire balance for monies due for his/her family.

Retirement Plan

It is our intent to offer a SIMPLE IRA plan effective no later than_____(month/day), 20____. Once the plan is established, the EMPLOYER will match EMPLOYEE contributions up to 3% of the EMPLOYEE'S annual salary. It will be the EMPLOYEES responsibility to determine the method in which these monies will be invested.

Vacation

EMPLOYER agrees to allow the EMPLOYEE to begin employment with two weeks of paid vacation beginning _____(month/ day), 20____. See the *Agency Employee Handbook* for additional vacation benefits and expectations.

Appendix D – Licensed CSR Employee Agreement

Individual Agreement

Licensed Customer Service Representative

_____, d/b/a, hereinafter called EMPLOYER, of ___address_____, and _____, d/b/a Customer Sales Representative hereinafter called EMPLOYEE, intending to be legally bound hereby, agree as follows:

This agreement will begin on ____ 1, 20__ and will end on December 31, 20__. At the conclusion of 20__, this compensation program may be amended.

EMPLOYER and EMPLOYEE shall be associated as EMPLOYER and EMPLOYEE at the rate of compensation as follows: **EMPLOYER shall pay EMPLOYEE the base sum of $__ per hour.** Payments will be made on or around the first and the fifteenth of each month. In addition to the BASE pay, the EMPLOYER will pay the EMPLOYEE a bonus as outlined below:

- $5 for appointment that shows up in the office to review their policy
- $10 (once licensed) for every Auto policy sold as a result of appointment
- $20 (once licensed) for every Home policy sold as a result of appointment
- $30 (once licensed) for every Life policy sold as a result of appointment

The Bonus Pay will be paid on the fifteenth of every month.

Medical

The EMPLOYER will pay ____ of the employee base Medical Coverage as outlined in the Agency Employee Handbook. The EMPLOYEE may choose additional coverage's at his or her own cost.

Bonus

Holiday Bonus: Based on the overall bottom line results of the Agency, a Holiday bonus may or may not be rewarded in the month of December for each EMPLOYEE. It is the EMPLOYERS intent to offer this bonus when the results and cash flow are positive. This bonus is planned to be $1 for every Net Gain in Policies (PIF) from January through December of that year.

Retirement Plan

The EMPLOYER will match EMPLOYEE contributions up to 3% of the EMPLOYEES annual salary. It will be the EMPLOYEES responsibility to determine the method in which these monies will be invested.

Vacation

EMPLOYER agrees to allow EMPLOYEE to begin employment with 2 weeks of paid vacation beginning January 1, 20__. During the 5th year of employment, EMPLOYEE will receive an additional week of paid vacation as outlined in the Agency Employee Handbook.

Employee Responsibilities

a. Answer the phone on the first ring.
b. Provide excellent service to each and EVERY one of our customers.
c. Collect cash and promptly (within 24-hours) ACA the monies. Complete the deposit slip for the agent to deposit monies.

d. Collect information from customers which is necessary to quote auto and homeowners insurance. You CANNOT give quotes or discuss coverage options until you are licensed.

e. Identify cross-sales opportunities and give information to a licensed CSR. Opportunities include: change of address, phone number, birth of a child, change in job...

f. Scan critical data into the agency customer contact management system as instructed by Agent.

g. Pick-up and sort mail ever day before 10 a.m.

h. Complete the attached minimum expectation report before the 5th of every month.

i. Come prepared to every staff meeting and discuss current performance, opportunities and priorities for the week ahead.

APPENDIX E – INDIVIDUAL AGREEMENT LICENSED AGENCY PRODUCER

Individual Agreement Licensed Agency Producer

The first 90-Days of employment are considered a Probationary Period. During this time, the agency will closely monitor a new employee's performance. All benefits commence after successful completion of the 90-Day Probationary Period as describe in the Agency Employee Guide.

If, after the 90-Day Probationary Period, an employee's performance is considered marginal, the EMPLOYER may extend the introductory period or terminate this Agreement all together. The _____ Insurance Agency reserves the right to do either at its own discretion.

AFTER SUCCESSFUL COMPLETION OF PROBATIONARY PERIOD

_____, d/b/a Agent, hereinafter called EMPLOYER, of ___ address_____, and _____, d/b/a Agency Producer hereinafter called EMPLOYEE, intending to be legally bound hereby, agree as follows:

This agreement will begin on _____ and will end on December 31, ___. At the conclusion of 20__, this compensation program may be amended. Although the base salary is likely to be the same in 20__, the bonus plan may change.

EMPLOYER and EMPLOYEE shall be associated as EMPLOYER and EMPLOYEE at the rate of compensation as follows: **EMPLOYER shall pay EMPLOYEE 50% new business commissions on all business brought in to the agency by the Agency Producer.**

Throughout this Agreement, the EMPLOYER guarantees the minimum salary for the EMPLOYEE to be $____ per month with the MAXIMUM base not to exceed $___. The first of the month, the EMPLOYEE will be paid $____ on or around the 1st of the month. The second paycheck will be made on or around the fifteenth of the month and will include the additional compensation (if any) with a minimum guarantee of $___. It is the EMPLOYEES responsibility to complete the EMPLOYEES PERFORMANCE REPORT (attached) and turn it in to the Office Manager on or before the 5th of every month.

In addition to the BASE pay, the EMPLOYER will pay the EMPLOYEE a bonus as outlined below:

Bonus

Holiday Bonus: Based on the overall bottom line results of the Agency, a Holiday bonus may or may not be rewarded in the month of December for each EMPLOYEE. It is the EMPLOYERS intent to offer this bonus when the results and cash flow are positive. This bonus is planned to be $1 for every policy-in-force growth (PIF) in the agency. For employees who start employment during the middle of the calendar year, the PIF at the time of employment will be used to determine the final end of year results.

Life Insurance Bonus: Because life insurance production is critical to our overall success, each employee will be reward for outstanding life insurance results. Each employee in the Agency will be compensated in the same manner for life insurance production:

1. For _____ – Every employee earns $100 bonus

2. For _____ – Every employee earns $250 bonus

3. For _____ – Every employee earns $500 bonus

Retirement Plan

The EMPLOYER will match EMPLOYEE contributions up to 3% of the EMPLOYEES annual salary. It will be the EMPLOYEES responsibility to determine the method in which these monies will be invested.

Health Insurance

The EMPLOYER will contribute up to $____ per month to the EMPLOYEES base medical plan.

Minimum Expectations

Every employee of the _____ Agency, Inc. will be required to produce an acceptable business result. With an employee focusing on producing __product type____ Insurance, it is expected that the employees in the agency produce a minimum of ____ with a Targeted Goal set at____. **Failure to issue at least 5 new business policies per month for 2-consecutive months could result in the termination of this agreement.**

_____	_____	_____	_____
Producer Name	Date	Agent Name	Date
Agency Producer		Agent	

APPENDIX F – INDIVIDUAL AGREEMENT COMMERCIAL SPECIALIST

Individual Agreement Commercial Specialist

The first 90-Days of employment are considered a Probationary Period. During this time, agency will closely monitor a new Employee's performance. All benefits commence after successful completion of the 90-Day Probationary Period as describe in the Agency Office Employee Guide.

If, after the 90-Day Probationary Period, the EMPLOYEE's performance is considered marginal, the EMPLOYER may extend the introductory period or terminate this Agreement all together. The [your name] Insurance Agency reserves the right to do either at its own discretion.

AFTER SUCCESSFUL COMPLETION OF PROBATIONARY PERIOD

[your agency name], hereinafter called EMPLOYER (or Agent), of [your address], and (name), d/b/a Commercial Specialist hereinafter called EMPLOYEE (or CS), intending to be legally bound hereby, agree as follows:

This agreement will begin on   (date) , 20__ and will end on   (date)   , 20__. At the conclusion of 20___, this compensation program may be amended. Although the base salary is likely to be the same in 20___, the bonus plan may change.

EMPLOYER and CS shall be associated as EMPLOYER and CS at the rate of compensation as follows: **EMPLOYER shall pay CS 50% of the Commercial New Business commissions generated by the CS. Commercial New Business Commissions consists of the following categories:**

- **Commercial P&C**
- **Commercial WC**

Throughout this Agreement, the EMPLOYER guarantees the minimum salary for the CS to be $____ per month. The first of the month, the CS will be paid $_____ on or around the 1st of the month. The second paycheck will be made on or around the fifteenth of the month and will include the additional compensation (if any) with a minimum guarantee of $____. It is the EMPLOYEES responsibility to complete the EMPLOYEE PERFORMANCE REPORT (attached) and turn it in to the Office Manager on or before the 5th of every month.

Conditions for Continuation of Guarantee and Performance Standards

Guaranteed Income Payments will continue provided the CS produces the minimum standards pursuant to the requirements below:

Three Month Requirement		Accumulated Requirement	
Quarter	Comrcl NB Commissions	Quarter	Comrcl NB Commissions
1st Q 20___	$6,000	1st Q 20___	$6,000
2nd Q 20___	$7,500	2nd Q 20___	$13,500
3rd Q 20___	$10,000	3rd Q 20___	$23,500
4th Q 20___	$12,000	4th Q 20___	$35,500
20___ +	$12,000	20___ +	$48,000 per year

If the Commercial Specialist fails to meet these Three-Month or Accumulated Requirements, the Agency will discontinue Guaranteed Income Payments to CS immediately.

1. Failure to Achieve Performance Standards

If the Guaranteed Income has been discontinued for failure to meet the performance standards under the Three-Month or Accumulated Requirements described in the paragraph above, the CS may be terminated for failure to achieve an acceptable business result.

If the Agent and CS mutually agree to continue the business agreement as outlined in this Agreement after the Guaranteed Income has been discontinued, the rate of compensation during the remaining 24-months of this contract to the CS will be as follows:

75% of the Commercial NB Commission generated by the CS for that Calendar Month

2. Reinstatement of Guaranteed Income

If after the Guaranteed Income has been discontinued for failure to meet the acceptable performance standards and the CS meets the next Three-Month and Accumulated Requirements, the Guaranteed Income payments will be reinstated starting the month after the requirements have been met, but not retroactively for amounts withheld from CS.

In addition to the BASE pay, the EMPLOYER will pay the CS a bonus as outlined below:

Bonus

Holiday Bonus: Based on the overall bottom line results of the Agency, a Holiday bonus may or may not be rewarded in the month of December for each employee. It is the EMPLOYERS intent to offer this bonus when the results and cash flow are positive. This bonus is planned to be $1 policy-in-force growth in the

Agency. PIF Growth is defined as the number of policies in the Agency on December 31st minus the policies in force on January 1st of that year (or at the start of employment). Policies assigned or purchased in the Agency are not included for bonus purposes.

List other bonus opportunities here.

Retirement Plan

The EMPLOYER will match CS contributions up to 3% of the employee's annual salary. It will be the EMPLOYEES responsibility to determine the method in which these monies will be invested.

Health Insurance

The EMPLOYER will contribute up to $___ per month to the CSS base medical plan.

Name	Date	Agent Name	Date
Commercial Specialist		Owner	

APPENDIX G – OFFICE MANAGER EMPLOYEE AGREEMENT

Office Manager Individual Employment Agreement

_____ , DBA, hereinafter called EMPLOYER, of _____ (address), and _____, DBA Customer Sales Representative hereinafter called EMPLOYEE, intending to be legally bound hereby, agree as follows:

This agreement will begin on_____(month/day), **20___ and will end on** _____ (month/day), **20___.** At the conclusion of 20___ this compensation program may be amended.

EMPLOYER and EMPLOYEE shall be associated as EMPLOYER and EMPLOYEE at the rate of compensation as follows: **EMPLOYER shall pay EMPLOYEE the base sum of $1,500 per month.** Payments will be made on or around the first and the fifteenth of each month.

Performance Bonuses

In addition to the BASE pay, the EMPLOYER will pay the EMPLOYEE a bonus on the fifteenth of the month as outlined below:

- $5 for every policy issued through the agency (reflected by the New Business Folio Report)
- $100 for every Level I life bonus

- $200 for every Level II life bonus
- $500 for every Level III life bonus

Medical

The EMPLOYER will pay one-half of the employee base medical coverage as outlined in the *Agency Employee Handbook*. The EMPLOYEE may choose additional coverages at his/her own cost.

Holiday Bonus

Based on the overall bottom line results of the Agency, a holiday bonus may or may not be rewarded in the month of December for each EMPLOYEE. It is the EMPLOYER'S intent to offer this bonus when the results and cash flow are positive. This bonus is planned to be $1 for every net gain in policies (PIF) from January through December of that year.

Retirement Plan

The EMPLOYER will match the EMPLOYEE's contributions up to 3% of the EMPLOYEE'S annual salary. It will be the EMPLOYEE'S responsibility to determine the method in which these monies will be invested.

Vacation

EMPLOYER agrees to allow EMPLOYEE to begin employment with two weeks of paid vacation beginning   (month/ day), 20 . During the 5th year of employment, EMPLOYEE will receive an additional week of paid vacation as outlined in the Agency Employee Handbook.

Employee Responsibilities

A. Develop an effective training program for all Agency employees.

B. Develop programs that are designed to educate and motivate staff to increase agent production.

C. Answer all incoming phone calls (2nd on the phone).

D. Handle insured complaints.

E. Update Agent production board and keep staff focused on goals and objectives of Agency.

F. Assist the Agent at all times.

APPENDIX H – RETENTION SPECIALIST AGREEMENT

Individual Agreement
Customer Retention Specialist

Agent Name, d/b/a Agent, hereinafter called EMPLOYER, of (address), and **Employee Name**, d/b/a Customer Retention Specialist hereinafter called EMPLOYEE, of _____ intending to be legally bound hereby, agree as follows:

This agreement will take effect on _____, 20__.

EMPLOYER and EMPLOYEE shall be associated as EMPLOYER and EMPLOYEE at the rate of compensation as follows: **EMPLOYER shall pay EMPLOYEE the sum of $___ per hour.**

In addition, after 90-days of employment, the EMPLOYER agrees to pay one-half of the EMPLOYEES monthly medical insurance premiums if the EMPLOYEE participates in the Agency medical insurance program. The EMPLOYEE will pay one-half of his/her medical insurance premiums and the entire balance for monies due for his/her family.

Bonus

Because the Customer Retention Specialist will play a key role in the overall success of the Agency, the EMPLOYEE will be compensated for successful performance. The bonus plan will be paid as follows:

MONTHLY

- $10 for every P&C appointment set by the EMPLOYEE (appointment must show-up)
- $20 for every life appointment set by the EMPLOYEE (appointment must show-up)

ANNUAL

- $1 for every PIF gain in the agency.

Retirement Plan

It is our intent to offer a SIMPLE IRA plan effective no later than _____, 20__. Once the plan is established, the EMPLOYER will match EMPLOYEE contributions up to 3% of the EMPLOYEES annual salary. It will be the EMPLOYEES responsibility to determine the method in which these monies will be invested.

Vacation

EMPLOYER agrees to allow EMPLOYEE to begin employment with 2 weeks of paid vacation beginning January 1, 20____. See the Agency Employee Handbook for addition vacation benefits and expectations.

Employee Responsibilities

a. Contact a minimum of 10 customers per hour. Thank them for their business and complete Customer Update Form.

b. Successfully administer the Emergency Contact and Neighborhood Watch Programs.

c. Collect information from customers which is necessary to quote auto and homeowners insurance. You CANNOT give quotes or discuss coverage options until you are licensed.

d. Identify cross-sales opportunities and give information to a licensed CSR. Opportunities include: change of address, phone number, birth of a child, change in job…

e. Scan critical data into the agency contact management system as instructed by Agent.

APPENDIX I - EMPLOYEE PERFORMANCE REPORT: AGENCY PRODUCER

Name_____ – Agency Producer

Production Month: _____

(Payment will be on the 15th of the Month
Following the Production Month)

P&C NB Commissions:	Life NB Commissions:	Total NB Commercial Commissions:	50% of Total NB Commissions:

Minimum 15th Paycheck = $_____

Total to Be Paid on the 15th: _____

Appendix J - Employee Performance Report: Commercial Specialist

Name_____ – Commercial Specialist

Production Month: _____

(Payment will be on the 15th of the Month
Following the Production Month)

Comrcl PC NB Commissions	Comrcl PC NB Commissions	Total NB Commercial Commissions:	50% of Total NB Commissions:

Minimum 15th Paycheck = $_____

Total to Be Paid on the 15th: _____

YEAR: 20__

Three Month Requirement			Accumulated Requirement		
Month	NB Actual	NB Required	NB Actual	NB Required	Over or Under
1		$2,000		$2,000	
2		$2,000		$4,000	
3		$2,000		$6,000	
1st Quarter		$6,000		$6,000	
4		$2,500		$8,500	
5		$2,500		$11,000	
6		$2,500		$13,500	
2nd Quarter		$7,500		$13,500	
7		$3,000		$16,500	
8		$3,000		$19,500	
9		$3,000		$22,500	
3rd Quarter		$9,000		$22,500	
10		$4,000		$26,500	
11		$4,000		$30,500	
12		$4,000		$34,500	
4th Quarter		$12,000		$34,500	

In 20___ and beyond, the minimum quarterly standard will be $4,000 per quarter and $48,000 per year.

APPENDIX K - EMPLOYEE PERFORMANCE REVIEW

EMPLOYEE INFORMATION

Name Of Employee Being Reviewed::	Reviewer's Name:
Date:	Review Period: ___ Quarter 20___

REVIEW GUIDELINES

Complete this personal review, using the following scale:

NA = Not Applicable   3 = Meets Requirements

1 = Unsatisfactory   4 = Exceeds Requirements

2 = Marginal   5 = Exceptional

EVALUATION

1.	Job Knowledge and Expertise					
2.	Ability and Dedication to Learn new tasks.					
3.	Uses Resources (ie. Company employees) in an effective manner.					
4.	Positive Attitude about office conditions.					
5.	Attendance Requirements					
6.	Takes responsibility for achievements and failures.					
7.	Tries new things and always looks for ways to add value to the team.					
8.	Listens to Direction from Management.					
9.	Generates creative ideas and solutions.					
10.	Brings in more revenue to the business that earns in payroll (Profit or Loss).					

Additional Comments: See next page.

My strengths are:

My weaknesses that need to be improved upon are:

I contribute to the team in the following ways:

I understand that i must bring in revenue to the business to justify my position on a daily basis. Over the last quarter, I have done the following things to bring in additional revenue for this business:

If I were to ask my team members about my performance, attitude and willingness to help them on a daily basis, I think they would say:

I have the following suggestions to improve the performance of our team:

APPENDIX L – AGENCY EMPLOYEE HANDBOOK

Note: This Agreement is for illustrative purposes only. You should seek legal assistance when preparing any type of document to make certain you are abiding to all state and federal laws governing employee conduct.

Agency Employee Handbook
Name of Agent
Updated: Current Date

Introduction

This handbook is intended to help you get acquainted with the_____Agency and describes, in general terms, some of our employment guidelines. This handbook should serve as a useful reference, even though it is not intended to be an official policy and procedure manual. Please understand that the handbook is not intended to be a contract (expressed or implied), nor is it intended to otherwise create any legally enforceable obligations on the part of the Agent/Owner. This handbook supersedes and replaces all previous personnel policies, practices and guidelines.

To obtain information regarding specific employment policies and procedures, whether or not they are referred to in this handbook, speak with the Agent. Because the Agency is a growing and changing organization, the Agent reserves full discretion to add to, modify or delete items without advance notice. For this reason, we urge you to check with the Agent to obtain current information regarding the status of any particular policy, procedure or practice. No individual other than the Agent has the authority to enter into any employment or other agreement that modifies Agency policy.

Equal Employment Opportunity Policy

Equal Employment Opportunity (EEO) is the right of all persons to be free from unlawful forms of discrimination in employment. The Agency recognizes and honors this right through our employment policy.

Hiring, promotions, salary adjustments, on the job training, and other decisions affecting terms and conditions of employment depend solely on merit, qualifications and competency. In addition, it is our intention to provide a work environment free of abusive, disrespectful or otherwise non-professional conduct. Members of the Agency shall not discriminate against any applicant or employee because of race, religious creed, color, sex, national origin, ancestry, age, disability or other bases protected by law.

Employee Harassment

The Agency is committed to providing a work environment which is free from unlawful forms of discrimination. In keeping with this commitment, the Agency maintains a strict policy prohibiting harassment or intimidation in any form including verbal, physical and visual, or any conduct which might be construed as a racial, sexual, ethnic or religious slur. These are serious violations of this policy and will not be condoned or permitted.

Sexual harassment includes, but is not limited to, making unwelcome sexual advances and request for sexual favors where:

1. Submission to such conduct is made an explicit or implicit term or condition of employment, or

2. Submission to or rejection of such conduct by an individual is used as the basis for employment decisions affecting such individual, or

3. Such conduct has the purpose or effect of substantially interfering with an individual's work performance or creating an intimidating, hostile, or offensive work environment.

Any employee who feels harassed by anyone in the Agency, or those doing business with the Agency should immediately bring the situation to the attention of the Agent. All such matters will be treated with confidentiality.

Employment At-Will Policy

All employment at the Agency is "at-will." That means that both employees and the Agency have the right to terminate employment at any time, with or without advance notice, and with or without cause. No one other than the Agent has the authority to alter this arrangement, and any such changes must be in writing.

Confidentiality

The nature of our business requires that much of what we do is kept confidential. In order to maintain the confidentiality of matters pertaining to our Agency, and the agents must take particular care in both business and personal conversations.

Specific Policies

1. Avoid discussions of our Agency's affairs with third parties unless you have been authorized to do so by the Agent.

2. Avoid discussions about our Agency's activities and our Customer's in public places such as restaurants, social functions, etc.

3. Refer any requests for information regarding the agency, agents, policyholder, employees and former employees to the Agent.

Customer-Needs Marketing Approach

The Agency is committed to Customer-Needs Marketing. This means we look to provide complete coverage to the Agency Force and tailor our service to meet their needs. Since this is our basic approach to doing business, it is part of everyone's job to provide this type of service. This starts with providing excellent customer service to all of our customers.

Attendance Policy

Clearly, good attendance is good for you and good for the Agency. It helps you achieve your own goals and objectives, and, in turn, helps you contribute to the Agency success. It is understood that there may be times when you may not be able to come to work, or may not be able to report on time. The following guidelines have been established to help you manage these situations.

Absences will be monitored on a rolling twelve-month basis, measuring back through the previous twelve months from the most current absence. Excessive absenteeism is defined as "eight or more days of chargeable absences in a rolling twelve-month period." For the purposes of any portion of a day taken off, an occurrence will be counted when any partial days within the rolling twelve months add up to one day. For example, two half days of chargeable absences will count as one occurrence.

Some absences are protected by law or are approved by the Agency and will not be charged as an occurrence. These non-chargeable absences include state protected family/medical/parental leaves, personal business leaves that have prior approval and are at the convenience of the department, e.g., jury duty, required court appearances, occupational injuries or illnesses, religious holidays and catastrophic conditions.

If you are unable to report for work, notify the Agent within one hour of your regularly scheduled starting time on each day you are absent unless your absence has been already approved for a specified time frame. *If you do not call when you are absent, and do not make contact with the Agent within the first hour on the second consecutive day of absence, it will be presumed that you have resigned from the company without notice.* You will then be removed from the payroll as of the last day you worked.

If you are absent for more than two (2) days, upon returning to work you must have a release from your doctor stating that you may return and resume your regular duties. The Agent may, however, request such a release after any absence as may be appropriate to assure the safety of you, your coworkers and the Agency.

Just as it is important to be at work each day, it is also important to be on time for work. If you are going to be late, let the Agent know as far in advance as possible. Tardiness, not being at work at your regularly scheduled time, will be monitored on a rolling twelve- month basis, just like absences. Excessive tardiness is defined as "six or more instances of being late in a rolling twelve-month period."

All absences, chargeable and non-chargeable, including partial time off, will be recorded. If the employee accumulates too many chargeable absences or tardies, progressive discipline may be implemented. Excessive absenteeism is defined as "eight or more changeable absences within a twelve-month rolling period), or excessive tardiness (defined as six or more instances of being late in a twelve-month rolling period) may result in further progressive discipline, up to and including termination of employment. A good attendance record enhances your ability to contribute to the Agency's results, and will directly affect potential salary treatment and future job opportunities.

Perfect Attendance will be rewarded in the Agency. Perfect Attendance is defined as "having one full calendar year of no partial or full-day absences and no more than one tardy." For each calendar year of perfect attendance, each employee will be rewarded with an additional day of vacation to be taken in the following year. In addition, the number of consecutive perfect attendance days will carry over for each year to a maximum of five (5). For example, 4 consecutive perfect attendance years = 4 additional days of vacation the following year. After having one full day absence or more than two tardies during a calendar year, the additional days of vacation rewarded will start back at zero.

Vacation, Sick Days, and Holidays

Sick Pay

Regular employees are eligible for sick pay benefits after (90) days with the Agency. Paid sick days will be limited to twenty-four hours per year for full-time employees and twelve hours per year for part- time employees.

Vacation

Regular full-time and part-time employees accrue paid vacation in accordance with the following:

Length of Employment	Vacation
2–4 years	2 weeks + sick time
5–14 years	3 weeks + sick time
15 years and up	4 weeks + sick time

Vacations shall be scheduled to provide adequate coverage of job responsibilities and staffing requirements. The office manager will make final determinations and must approve your vacation schedule in advance.

Employees on unpaid leave do not accrue vacation. Vacation time in years where unpaid leave is taken will be adjusted accordingly.

Holidays

The Agency observes the following paid holidays:

- New Year's Day
- Memorial Day (last Monday in May)
- Independence Day
- Labor Day
- Thanksgiving (Thursday and Friday)
- Christmas (in accordance with state office schedule)

When a holiday falls on Saturday, the previous Friday is observed as a holiday. When a holiday falls on Sunday, the following Monday is observed. The observance of holidays, other than those listed, will be announced by the Agent.

Telephone Policy Statement

Telephones are provided for Agency business use only. Each person who has a telephone is directly responsible for its use and care. Please minimize incoming or outgoing personal calls.

Employer reserves the right to periodically monitor business phones to ensure business use and proper telephone etiquette. Employees should, therefore, not assume that calls made or received on Agency lines are confidential.

Voicemail

Voicemail should be used only as a last resort when the entire office is in a meeting or it is not possible to answer an incoming call. Each office staff member, regardless of position, is responsible for assisting in the phone duties and should make every attempt to ensure that all phone calls are answered quickly and courteously. The Agent will assign phone responsibilities to each employee. You should check your voicemail frequently and return calls at the earliest possible time. If you will be unavailable for an extended period of time, it is your responsibility to change your personal greeting.

Employee Safety

Your safety is a primary concern of everyone in our organization. The following safety guidelines should be followed:

- If you become injured while working, no matter how slight, report your injuries to the Agent.
- Report unsafe conditions to the Agent immediately.

Normal Work Schedule

The Agency's normal business hours are from 8:00 A.M. until 6:00 P.M., Monday, Wednesday and Friday and 8:00 A.M. until 7:30 P.M. on Tuesday and Thursday. Employees are expected to take shifts working every other Saturday from 10:00 A.M. until 2:00 PM. Employees working Saturdays will be given four hours of "flex-time" off during the same work week. Flex time cannot be accumulated.

The Agent will assign your individual work schedule. Employees working over six hours in one day will be provided an unpaid lunch break approximately in the middle of the workday. Employees are allowed fifteen-minute rest periods for every four hours worked or major portion thereof. Your Agent will schedule your lunch.

Time Cards

All non-exempt employees are required to complete weekly time cards in ink, showing the actual time worked each day.

Pay Days

Employees are paid twice a month—on the 15th and the last day of every month, or on the preceding workday whenever a scheduled payday falls on Saturday, Sunday or a holiday. Mandatory federal, state and city deductions will be withheld from each paycheck.

Professional Appearance

The public gains many of its impressions of a company from its contact with its employees; therefore, personal appearance can create favorable or unfavorable impressions. We ask each employee to observe good habits of grooming and personal hygiene. Employees are expected to dress in appropriate business attire that reflects good judgment and taste.

Compensation Review

All full-time employees of the Agency will have their performance review on an annual basis and more often, at the employer's discretion, when work performance warrants special consideration. The annual reviewed will be scheduled in January of each year. Depending on the outcome of this review, compensation may be adjusted. Your employer will evaluate you on your job proficiency, chargeable absences, initiative, productivity and cooperation, plus any noteworthy accomplishments during the year using the following schedule outlined below.

You should come to the review session prepared with your own self-appraisal for these job areas. The Agency can only be successful by having competent, courteous and effective employees. The two purposes of this annual review are to help you improve your performance and to reward good performance.

Each full-time employee will be given a maximum   % increase in their annual base pay (up to a salary maximum) **unless on a pay- for-performance plan.**

Hourly Non-Exempt Employee Annual Performance Plan

Job Area Pay Increase

Job Knowledge and Quality	0, 1%, 2%
Positive Attitude and Cooperation	0, 1%, 2%

Job Proficiency and Productivity	0, 1%
Initiative and Creativity	0, 1%

Absences Pay Increase

0 occurrence	+4%
1 occurrence	+2%
2 occurrences	+1%
3 occurrences	+0%
4 occurrences	-1%
5 occurrences	-3%
6 occurrences or more	-5%

Salary Maximums

In an effort to maintain a competitive salary scale, it is the intention of the Agent to make annual salary adjustments which are higher than the industry average. However, due to the potential large annual salary increase, there will be a time when an employee's salary must be capped for each position. The salary cap will make it possible for additional employees to be hired and the creation of new job opportunities. After the salary cap is obtained, it is the Agent's intention to offer additional performance bonuses to motivate employees to perform at maximum potential. The salary range for each full-time employee/contract position is as follows:

Full-Time/Contract Salary Plan

Job Title Salary Range

Receptionist	$ 7–$10.00 per hour
Telemarketer	$ 7–$10.00 per hour + bonus
Administrative Assistant	$ 8–$14.00 per hour
Retention Specialist	$1,200–$2,000 monthly

Licensed CSR	1,200–$2,500 monthly + bonus
Office Manager	contract
Commercial Specialist	contract
Agency Producer	contract

Non-Monetary Compensation

In addition to salary benefits, full-time employees who have **less than three (3) occurrences (absences)** during the past twelve months and have maintained continuous employment for the Agency will receive the following benefits:

Three (3) Years Continuous Employment (choose one)

- Maid service (bi-monthly)
- Yard service (monthly)
- Health club membership for one
- Two (2) additional days of vacation

Five (5) Years Continuous Employment (choose one)

- Maid service (weekly)
- Full yard service
- Health club membership for two
- Three (3) additional days of vacation

Ten (10) Years Continuous Employment (choose two)

- Maid service (weekly)
- Health club membership for two
- Yard Service (weekly)
- Five (5) additional days of vacation

Grievance Procedure

Any complaints or grievances should be brought to the attention of the Agent. We believe that only in the atmosphere of open two-way communication can we establish positive employee-employer relations. Employees with a grievance are encouraged to discuss their complaint or grievance verbally or in writing with the Agent.

Ethical Conduct

This Agency has built and consistently maintained a reputation for conducting its business affairs in accordance with the highest standard of integrity and ethical behavior. As a representative of this office, you will be expected to maintain this standard. You are expected to be honest and follow legal requirements in all your dealings with the Agent, others in the Agency, the agents reporting to the Agency, the customers and to others that deal with the Agency. Any illegal or dishonest behavior on the part of the employee is grounds for disciplinary action up to and including termination of employment.

Non-Compete Agreement

Employees of the Agency also agree, as a condition of employment, that they will not engage in competition with the Agency or the agents of the Agency upon termination with the Agency. Specifically, employees agree to neither directly, nor indirectly solicit, accept or service the insurance business of a policy holder of record in the Agency as of the date of termination for a period of one year following their date of termination.

Acceptance of Terms

After reading this Employee handbook, complete the form below and return it to the Agent.

This acknowledges that I have been given a copy of the *Agency Employee Handbook* summarizing the Agency's personnel guidelines. I have read and understand these guidelines and will comply with them. I understand the statements contained in the *Agency Employee Handbook* are not intended to create any contractual or other legal obligations. I also understand that in accordance with the Agency's procedures, any policies, benefits, or practices described in the *Agency Employee Handbook* may be modified or rescinded at any time without prior notice to me.

I also understand that employment at the Agency is "at-will," which means that both employees and the Agency have the right to terminate employment at any time, with or without advance notice or cause.

_____   _____

Employee Signature   Date

APPENDIX M - CUSTOMER UPDATE FORM

"Hello Mr. /Ms _____, this is _____ calling on behalf of your insurance agent _____. How are you today?

_____, wanted me to call you today to first of all, thank you for your business. Secondly, he wanted to let you know that we are reviewing your file and we want to make sure our information is correct and that you are getting all of the discounts you may be eligible for. Do you have a few minutes? (If not, get a good time to call back)

Great! One of the updates I wanted to let you know about is that you now have the ability to print your ID Cards and review other policy information now on-line. Would you like the ability to access your accounts and print ID cards from your home computer 24-hours a day? I will send you the link to your email address. What is your primary email address?

Name:					Home:		
Email:					Business:		
Preferred Method of Communication:					Cell:		

	Types of Policies with Our Company:		Auto	Home	Comrcl	Life	Other
	Question	Y	N	Comment			
1	Have there been any changes in your household that may require the need for your insurance policy to be reviewed? (like: change in job, birth or marriage)						
2	Are you familiar with our companies new life insurance discounts? You can save up to __% on your auto insurance premium if you have life insurance with _____. Many of our customers are surprised to see that some small term life insurance policies cost them under $10 per month. Would you like us to run a quick quote for you to see how much you could save?						

We are implementing an Emergency Contact program to make certain we can reach you in the event of a catastrophe. The key to getting claims adjusters out to your house quickly relies on our ability to communicate with you.

3	Can you give me the name and phone number of a relative or friend in the ___ area who can get in contact with you 24-hours a day?	Name:			Phone:		
4	I also need to get the name and phone number of a neighbor who would not mind checking your home for damage in the event you are out of town.	Name:			Phone:		
5	Because insurance is a large part of everyone's monthly budget, it's important that as your professional insurance agent, we sit down once every few years and make sure you have the coverage you need and have all of the discounts you may be eligible for. Would you like to come in to have _____ review your policy with you?						

Appendix N – Business Exit Interview

[company logo]
Business Exit Interview

Customer Name: _____   **Address:** _____

Date:_____   **City/State/Zip:** _____

Household Number: _____   **Employee Name:** _____

	Auto	Fire	Life	Comrcl	Other
Policy #					
NB Date					
Canc Date					

1	Poor
2	Fair
3	Good
4	Very Good
5	Excellent

For each item identified below, circle the number to the right that best fits your judgment of its quality. Use the scale above to select the quality number.

Description / Identification of Survey Item	Scale
1. How would you rate the overall service provided by our agency?	1 2 3 4 5
2. When you contacted our office, was the return call prompt and courteous?	Yes No
3. How would you rank our claims service?	1 2 3 4 5
4. How would you rank the quality of our products?	1 2 3 4 5
5. How would you rank the knowledge of our agency staff?	1 2 3 4 5
6. Would you recommend our agency to a friend?	Yes No
7. What could we have done differently to retain your business?	Yes No
8. May we periodically contact you to once again earn your business?	Yes No

What would you say the primary reason is for leaving our Agency:

▢ Price   ▢ Service   ▢ Products ▢ Relocation ▢ Other: _____

APPENDIX O - LIFE INSURANCE DECLINATION FORM

Life Insurance Declination Agreement

[LOGO]

(Please read carefully before signing)

Your Insurance Company Policy Number: _____

[Insert company-specific details about discounts or benefits provided by life cover- age.]

I have been given the opportunity to purchase Life Insurance and have elected to reject this coverage.

_____   _____

Signature of Named Insured   Date

Front of 7˝ x 5˝ Card

Life Insurance Declination Agreement

(Please read carefully before signing)

Important Notice

Your Homeowners policy #_____ provides for only those coverages described in the policy. These coverages pertain to property and liability. There is no coverage for the payoff of the mortgage in the event of death of the insured or spouse.

A policy is available to pay off the mortgage and leave the home free and clear in the event of the death of the insured or spouse of the household.

I have read and understand the above.

___ I desire more information on a Mortgage
    Protection Plan.

___ I do not desire any further information.

_____   _____

Signature of Named Insured   Date

Back of 7″ x 5″ Card

Appendix P – State Insurance Licensing Guidelines

State Insurance Licensing Guidelines

The following guidelines were provided by Kaplan Financial Education as of October 2012. Please check for updated requirements before scheduling your exam.

Kaplan Financial provides a single source for premier education and compliance solutions, bringing together leading brands to help customers accelerate speed to market, boost revenue and minimize risk. Over the last 70 years, Kaplan Financial Education has provided the most current test preparation and continuing education materials for Securities and Insurance professionals.

Kaplan's offerings include licensing exam prep, continuing education and firm element, wealth management, financial planning, insurance designation programs and compliance management tools and services. For more information, visit KaplanFinancial.com.

Alabama

Candidates for a producer license, either Life & Health or Property & Casualty, must attend a pre-licensing course for that line of authority consisting of forty (40) classroom hours or equivalent of individual instruction including a minimum of five hours dedicated to the discussion of Alabama law. Students may attend courses in the classroom or online. For candidates taking an online course, their final exam must be monitored by a disinterested third party (someone other than a relative, friend, or business associate).

Exams are administered by the Alabama State Department of Insurance and the University of Alabama College of Continuing Studies. For online registration and exam information, visit the Alabama Department of Insurance website at aldoi.gov or contact the University of Alabama College of Continuing Studies at 205-348-0633.

Alaska

Candidates for a Life & Health or Property & Casualty producer license are not required to complete pre-licensing education to sit for the state exam, but completing an exam preparation course can significantly increase the opportunity to pass on the first attempt.

Although pre-licensing education is not required, due to the difficulty and nature of these exams, Kaplan highly recommends enrolling in a study course. These exams are difficult to pass unless you spend a significant amount of time learning about the principles, products, and markets associated with today's dynamic insurance career. For more information about Kaplan Financial's study courses, visit KaplanFinancial.com. To schedule an exam, call Pearson VUE at 800-274-5993 or visit pearsonvue.com.

Arizona

Candidates are not required to complete pre-licensing education to sit for the state exam, but completing an exam preparation course can significantly increase the opportunity to pass on the first attempt.

Although pre-licensing education is not required, due to the difficulty and nature of these exams, Kaplan highly recommends enrolling in a study course. These exams are difficult to pass unless you spend a significant amount of time learning about the principles, products, and markets associated with today's dynamic insurance career. For more information about Kaplan Financial's study courses, visit KaplanFinancial.com. To obtain a Licensing Information Bulletin or schedule an exam, call Prometric at 800-853-5448 or visit prometric.com.

Arkansas

Applicants must complete 20 hours of pre-licensing education for a Life license, 20 hours for an Accident/Health/Sickness license, 20 hours for Property, 20 hours for Casualty and 20 hours for Personal Lines. Although the majority of the pre-licensing course must be completed through classroom education, up to five (5) hours may be completed by electronic media.

Applicants may not schedule a test without an examination permit in hand. You can obtain this permit (good for only 90 days) by submitting the completed application and fee to Pearson VUE.

To get the *Licensing Exam Candidate Handbook*, visit pearsonvue.com. To schedule an exam, contact Pearson Vue at 888-204-6259 once you have received your examination permit.

California

Pre-licensing education requirements include 20 hours for Life, 20 hours for Accident and Health, 40 hours for Life/Accident & Health, 40 hours for Property & Casualty and 20 hours for Personal Lines. All candidates are required to complete 12 hours of approved pre-licensing classroom study on Ethics and the California Insurance Code. For online registration and exam information, visit PSI Exams Online at psiexams.com or call 877-392-6422.

Colorado

Candidates must earn 50 hours of pre-licensing education for each full resident license. Each license requires ten (10) hours on principles of insurance, legal concepts and regulations, and ethics plus pre-licensing education in a specific line: 40 hours of Life, 40 hours of Health, 40 hours of Property & Casualty and 40 hours of Personal Lines

Pre-licensing education requirements may be met through classroom attendance, an approved correspondence self-study program or online. Self-study courses must have a final exam that is monitored by a disinterested third party. Classroom courses exams must be monitored by a qualified instructor. To obtain a *Licensing Exam Candidate Handbook* or schedule an exam, call Pearson VUE at 800-274-2616 or visit pearsonvue.com.

Connecticut

Applicants for a producer license must complete pre-licensing education courses in the classroom, online or through an approved correspondence self-study program, as follows: 40 hours for Life, 40 hours for Accident & Health, 80 hours for Life/Accident & Health, 80 hours for Property & Casualty and 40 hours for Personal Lines.

All candidates are required to bring the original pre-license course certificate to the test center on examination day. Candidates show the certificate at the test center and then submit the certificate with their license application. Pre-licensing course certificates are valid for one year from the completion date. To obtain a *Licensing Information Bulletin* or schedule an exam, call Prometric at 800-341-3257 or visit prometric.com.

Delaware

Candidates are not required to complete pre-licensing education to sit for the state exam, but completing an exam preparation course can significantly increase the opportunity to pass on the first attempt.

Although pre-licensing education is not required, due to the difficulty and nature of these exams, Kaplan highly recommends enrolling in a study course. These exams are difficult to pass unless you spend a significant amount of time learning about the principles, products, and markets associated with today's dynamic insurance career. For more information about Kaplan Financial's study courses, visit KaplanFinancial.com. To obtain a *Licensing Exam Candidate Handbook* or schedule an exam, call Pearson VUE at 800-274-0455 or visit pearsonvue.com.

District of Columbia

Candidates are not required to complete pre-licensing education to sit for the state exam, but completing an exam preparation course can significantly increase the opportunity to pass on the first attempt.

Although pre-licensing education is not required, due to the difficulty and nature of these exams, Kaplan highly recommends enrolling in a study course. These exams are difficult to pass unless you spend a significant amount of time learning about the principles, products, and markets associated with today's dynamic insurance career. For more information about Kaplan Financial's study courses, visit KaplanFinancial.com.

To obtain a *Licensing Exam Candidate Handbook* or schedule an exam, call Pearson VUE at 800-274-0610 or visit pearsonvue.com.

Florida

Candidates must complete 40 hours for Life & Variable, 40 hours for Health, 40 hours for Life, Health and Variable, 200 hours for General Lines (Property & Casualty) and 52 hours for Personal Lines, all of which must include three (3) hours on the subject of Ethics. This course work can be completed in the classroom, online or as part of a self-study program. The final exam for self-study courses must be monitored by a disinterested third party.

Pearson VUE handles the entire examination process, including fees. Applicants do not need to apply with the Florida Department of Insurance and become authorized before taking the exam, except for bail bond applicants. There will no longer be any Exam-Only applications, as applicants may take the exam as many times as they like before they apply with the department.

To get a *Licensing Exam Candidate Handbook* or schedule an exam, call Pearson VUE at 888-274-2020 or visit pearsonvue.com.

Georgia

Applicants must complete 20 hours for Life, 20 hours for Accident and Sickness, 40 hours for Property & Casualty, 20 hours for Personal Lines and eight (8) hours for Variable Products (plus life insurance license). Course work may be completed in the classroom or online. Applicants must pass the required examination for licensure within 12 months of completion of the pre-licensing course. Those who fail to pass the exam after taking it three times must take another pre-licensing course before retaking the exam.

To obtain a *Licensing Exam Candidate Handbook* or schedule an exam, call Pearson VUE at 800-274-0488 or visit pearsonvue.com.

Hawaii

Candidates are not required to complete pre-licensing education to sit for the state exam, but completing an exam preparation course can significantly increase your odds of passing on the first attempt.

Although pre-licensing education is not required, due to the difficulty and nature of these exams, Kaplan highly recommends enrolling in a study course. These exams are difficult to pass unless you spend a significant amount of time learning about the principles, products, and markets associated with today's dynamic insurance career. For more information about Kaplan Financial's study courses, visit KaplanFinancial.com.

To obtain a *Licensing Exam Candidate Handbook* or schedule an exam, call Pearson VUE at 800-274-2608 or visit pearsonvue.com.

Idaho

Candidates are not required to complete pre-licensing education to sit for the state exam, but completing an exam preparation course can significantly increase your odds of passing on the first attempt.

Although pre-licensing education is not required, due to the difficulty and nature of these exams, Kaplan highly recommends enrolling in a study course. These exams are difficult to pass unless you spend a significant amount of time learning about the principles, products, and markets associated with today's dynamic insurance career. For more information about Kaplan Financial's study courses, visit KaplanFinancial.com.

To obtain a *Licensing Exam Candidate Handbook* or schedule an exam, call Pearson VUE at 888-204-6218 or visit pearsonvue.com.

Illinois

Candidates must complete a total of 20 hours for Life, 20 hours for Accident/Health, 40 hours for Property & Casualty and 20 hours for Personal Lines. Courses must be taken through class or through an approved correspondence self-study program, but 7.5 hours must be completed in a classroom setting. Candidates will be required to show proof of pre-licensing completion at the test center before they will be allowed to take the exam. Pre-licensing education certificates are valid for one year from the date of completion.

To get a *Licensing Exam Candidate Handbook* or schedule an exam, call Pearson VUE at 800-274-0402 or visit pearsonvue.com. Applicants should allow five days after taking the Illinois state exam before applying for the state license.

Indiana

Applicants for producer licenses are required to complete pre-licensing education in the classroom, online or through a self-study program. The required hours are as follows: 40 hours for Life & Health, 20 hours for Life, 20 hours for Health, 40 hours for Property & Casualty and 20 hours for Personal Lines. Candidates taking an online course are required to track their online study time. In order to successfully complete the course, you must complete the required number of hours while studying in the Course Contents Units of the online course. Your online course tracker will be displayed in the upper right hand corner of your page so you can verify the time spent. At the end of the study course, the education provider will issue the Certificate of Completion, which is valid for six months. Applicants must present the original Certificate of Completion at the test center on the day of the exam.

To obtain a *Licensing Information Bulletin,* call PAN at 877-449-8378 or visit panpowered.com. To register and schedule an exam, visit panpowered.com.

Iowa

Candidates are not required to complete pre-licensing education to sit for the state exam, but completing an exam preparation course can significantly increase your odds of passing on the first attempt.

Although pre-licensing education is not required, due to the difficulty and nature of these exams, Kaplan highly recommends enrolling in a study course. These exams are difficult to pass unless you spend a significant amount of time learning about the principles, products, and markets associated with today's dynamic insurance career. For more information about Kaplan Financial's study courses, visit KaplanFinancial.com.

To obtain a *Licensing Exam Candidate Handbook* or schedule an exam, call Pearson VUE at 877-540-5825 or visit pearsonvue.com.

Kansas

Candidates are not required to complete pre-licensing education to sit for the state exam, but completing an exam preparation course can significantly increase your odds of passing on the first attempt.

Although pre-licensing education is not required, due to the difficulty and nature of these exams, Kaplan highly recommends enrolling in a study course. These exams are difficult to pass unless you spend a significant amount of time learning about the principles, products, and markets associated with today's dynamic insurance career. For more information about Kaplan Financial's study courses, visit KaplanFinancial.com.

To obtain a *Licensing Exam Candidate Handbook* or schedule an exam, call Pearson VUE at 888-204-6255 or visit pearsonvue.com.

Kentucky

Candidates are required to complete 40 hours for Life and Health, 40 hours for Property & Casualty and 20 hours for Personal Lines. Course work may be completed in the classroom, online or through a self-study program. The final exam for self-study courses must be monitored by a disinterested third party. Candidates taking an online course are required to track their online study time. In order to successfully complete the course, you must complete the required number of hours while studying in the Course Contents Units of the online course. Your online course tracker will be displayed in the upper right hand corner of your page so you can verify the time spent.

For licensing information or to schedule an exam, visit the Kentucky Department of Insurance website at doi.ppr.ky.gov. To schedule an exam, click on "eServices" in the upper right-hand corner and set up an account.

There is no limit on the number of times applicants may retake an exam. The insurance application remains valid for 120 days, and upon payment of the examination retake fee, the applicant may reschedule and complete an exam as many times as they would like within this 120-day period. http://www.kfeducation.com/insurance-lic/

Louisiana

Candidates are required to complete pre-licensing education in a classroom. The hours are: Life (16 hours); Health & Accident (16 hours); Life, Health & Accident (32 hours); Property (32 hours); Casualty (32 hours); Property & Casualty (32 hours); Bail Bond (8 hours); Personal Lines (32 hours) included in Property & Casualty.

To get a *Licensing Information Bulletin* or schedule an exam, call Thomson Prometric (formerly Experior Assessments) at 1-800-871-6457. Go to their website at prometric.com for the bulletin and details.

Maine

Resident candidates for the Life & Health and Property & Casualty producers license are required to have a minimum of six (6) months experience in the insurance industry and an affidavit signed by the employer, or must complete sixteen (16) hours of approved instruction and receive a certificate of completion. Courses may be taken in class or through an approved correspondence self-study program.

To get *Licensing Information Bulletin* or schedule an exam, call Thomson Prometric (formerly Experior Assessments) at 1-800-853-5448. Go to their website at prometric.com for the bulletin, to register online, or to get more details.

Maryland

An applicant for a Life & Health license must meet one of the following criteria: (1) Satisfactory completion of a sixty-hour study course given by an approved/recognized school or course provider; or (2) One year employment by an insurer, producer or broker. Applicants for a Property & Casualty license must complete ninety-six (96) hours of study given by an approved/recognized school, or one year employment by an insurer or producer.

To get a *Licensing Examination Candidate Handbook* or schedule an exam, call Promissor at 1-800-274-2605. Go to their website at promissor.com for the handbook and details.

Massachusetts

Candidates are not required to complete pre-licensing education to sit for the state exam, but completing an exam preparation course can significantly increase the opportunity to pass on the first attempt.

Your state does not require specific education before you take the Life, Life & Health, or Property & Casualty exam to obtain a producer's license. However, Dearborn realizes that these exams are difficult to pass unless you spend a significant amount of time learning about the principles, products, and markets associated with today's dynamic insurance career. That's why we recommend enrolling with Dearborn in an exam prep course, which can be taken at one of Kaplan Financial's convenient classroom locations or through Kaplan Financial's self-study option available in text- book, online or webcast formats. You learn the important basics you will need to succeed on the state exam and succeed in your career. Feel free to contact Kaplan Financial at 800-521-3395 for more information about Kaplan Financial's programs, to order, or to enroll.

To get *Licensing Information Bulletin* or schedule an exam, call Thomson Prometric (formerly Experior Assessments) at 1-800-853-5448. Go to their website at prometric.com for the bulletin, to register online, or to get more details.

Michigan

The Michigan Insurance Code requires forty (40) hours of course work for both the property/casualty and life/health license. For a Life only license, twenty-six (26) hours of education are required (20 hours Life, 6 hours Michigan code); for a Health-only license, twenty (20) hours of course work are required (14 hours Health, 6 hours Michigan code). Courses may be taken in class or through an approved correspondence self-study program.

To get a *Licensing Exam Candidate Handbook* or schedule an exam, call Promissor at 1-800-274-2623. Go to their website at promissor. com for the handbook and more details.

Minnesota

Candidates are required to complete thirty (30) hours in Basic Fundamentals AND 7.5 hours in Life, 7.5 hours in Accident & Health, 7.5 hours in Property, 7.5 hours in Casualty, 7.5 hours in Personal Lines. All courses must be in a classroom.

To get a *Licensing Information Bulletin* or schedule an exam, call Thomson Prometric (formerly Experior Assessments) at 1-800-864-5312. Go to their website at prometric.com for the bulletin and more details.

Mississippi

Pre-licensing education requirements must be completed in a classroom. The hours required are: Life (12 hours), Health/Accident (12 hours); Life/Accident/Health (24 hours); Fire/Casualty (24 hours); Adjuster (12 hours); Bail Producer (8 hours).

All examinations are administered by: Testing Services, Inc. For details and registration form for the exam, go to the Mississippi Insurance Department website at doi.state.ms.us and view the licensing information and applications. Specific questions may be directed to the Licensing Division at 601-359-3569.

Missouri

Candidates are not required to complete pre-licensing education to sit for the state exam, but completing an exam preparation course can significantly increase the opportunity to pass on the first attempt.

Your state does not require specific education before you take the Life, Life & Health, or Property & Casualty exam to obtain a producer's license. However, Dearborn realizes that these exams are difficult to pass unless you spend a significant amount of time learning about the principles, products and markets associated with today's dynamic insurance career. That's why we recommend enrolling with Dearborn in an exam prep course. Options in your state may include a classroom location or through Kaplan Financial's self-study materials available in textbook, online or webcast formats. You learn the important basics you will need to succeed on the state exam and succeed in your career. Check the website for program availability, to order, and to enroll. Feel free to contact Kaplan Financial at 800-521-3395 for more information about Kaplan Financial's programs.

To get *Licensing Information Bulletin* or schedule an exam, call Thomson Prometric (formerly Experior Assessments) at 1-800-853-5448. Go to their website at prometric.com for the bulletin, to register online, or to get more details.

Montana

Candidates are not required to complete pre-licensing education to sit for the state exam, but completing an exam preparation course can significantly increase the opportunity to pass on the first attempt.

Your state does not require specific education before you take the Life, Life & Health, or Property & Casualty exam to obtain a producer's license. However, Dearborn realizes that these exams are difficult to pass unless you spend a significant amount of time learning about the principles, products and markets associated with today's dynamic insurance career. That's why we recommend enrolling with Dearborn in an exam prep course. Options in your state may include a classroom location or through Kaplan Financials self-study materials available in textbook, online or webcast formats. You learn the important basics you will need to succeed on the state exam and succeed in your career. Check the website for program availability, to order, and to enroll. Feel free to contact Kaplan Financial at 800-521-3395 for more information about Kaplan Financials programs.

To get a *Licensing Exam Candidate Handbook* or schedule an exam, call Promissor at 1-800-274-8906. Go to their website at promissor.com for the handbook and more details.

Nebraska

Candidates must complete education courses with at least six (6) hours of ethics PLUS education in the line of insurance: Life & Annuities license: 14 hours Life; Sickness, Accident & Health: 14 hours Health, including 6 hours of Medicare and LTC; Combined Life & Health: 17 hours Life, 17 Health (to include 6 hours of Medicare and LTC); Property & Casualty: 34 hours of Property & Casualty. Courses can be completed through class- room or an approved correspondence self-study program. There are also education requirements for Title, Assessment Association and Crop licenses.

To get Licensing Information Bulletin or schedule an exam, call Thomson Prometric (formerly Experior Assessments) at 1-800-853-4753. Go to their website at prometric.com for the bulletin and details.

Nevada

Candidates for a license in one line of insurance are required to complete twenty-five (25) hours in that line of insurance. Candidates for a license in Life and Health insurance or Property & Casualty insurance must complete thirty-five (35) hours in those lines. Candidates for a license in all lines of insurance must complete a sixty-five-hour course covering all lines of insurance. All courses include five (5) hours of state law requirement. Approved courses must be taken from a Nevada school, in class or through an approved correspondence self-study program.

To get a *Licensing Exam Candidate Handbook* or schedule an exam, call Promissor at 1-800-274-2609. Go to their website at Promissor.com for the handbook and more details.

New Hampshire

New applicants for a license must complete an approved course of pre-licensing education or meet a six-month experience requirement.

To get a *Licensing Information Bulletin* or schedule an exam, call Thomson Prometric (formerly Experior Assessments) at 1-800-869-6603. Go to their website at prometric.com for the bulletin and details.

New Jersey

Applicants must complete classroom instruction at a New Jersey-approved school. Hours are: Life (40); Health (40); Combined Life & Health (65); Property (55), Casualty (55); Combined Property & Casualty (95); Personal Lines (65); Title (60); Limited Lines Bail Bonds (10).

To get a *Licensing Exam Candidate Handbook* or schedule an exam, call Promissor at 1-800-274-7168. Go to their website at promissor.com for the handbook and more details.

New Mexico

Candidates are not required to complete pre-licensing education to sit for the state exam, but completing an exam preparation course can significantly increase the opportunity to pass on the first attempt.

Your state does not require specific education before you take the Life, Life & Health, or Property & Casualty exam to obtain a producer's license. However, Dearborn realizes that these exams are difficult to pass unless you spend a significant amount of time learning about the principles, products and markets associated with today's dynamic insurance career. That's why we recommend enrolling with Dearborn in an exam prep course. Options in your state may include a classroom location or through Kaplan Financials self-study materials available in textbook, online or webcast formats. You learn the important basics you will need to succeed on the state exam and succeed in your career. Check the website for program availability, to order and to enroll. Feel free to contact Kaplan Financial at 800-521-3395 for more information about Kaplan Financials programs.

To get a *Licensing Information Bulletin* or schedule an exam, call Thomson Prometric (formerly Experior Assessments) at 1-800-324-4689. Go to their website at prometric.com for the bulletin and details.

New York

Candidates for a producer license must have forty (40) hours of classroom education for Life and/or Accident & Health. For Property & Casualty, candidates need ninety (90) hours. Property & Casualty brokers must have ninety (90) hours of classroom education.

To get a *Licensing Exam Candidate Handbook* or schedule an exam, call Thomson Prometric (formerly Experior Assessments) at 1-800-324-7147. Go to their website at prometric.com for more details.

North Carolina

Applicants for Life & Health or Property & Casualty licenses must complete forty (40) hours of pre-licensing education. The education requirement can be satisfied through an approved correspondence self-study program, with a final exam proctored by an instructor, or classroom courses. Applicants for the Medicare Supplement/Long-Term Care exam must complete ten (10) hours of pre-licensing education.

Personal Lines license requires thirty-two (32) hours of pre-licensing education. To get a *Licensing Exam Candidate Handbook* or schedule an exam, call Promissor at 1-800-274-0668. Go to their website at promissor.com or the handbook and more details.

North Dakota

Candidates are required to take eight (8) hours of classroom pre-licensing education per line. That is, eight (8) hours each for: Life & Annuities; Accident & Health; Property; Casualty.

To get a *Licensing Information Bulletin* or schedule an exam, call Thomson Prometric (formerly Experior Assessments) at 1-800-861-9072. Go to their website at prometric.com for the bulletin and details.

Ohio

Candidates must complete a forty (40) hour classroom course for (1) Life, Accident & Health and Variable Products, and (2) Multiple Lines—Property & Casualty. Personal Lines candidates must complete twenty (20) hours of pre-licensing classroom education.

To get a *Licensing Information Bulletin* or schedule an exam, call Thomson Prometric (formerly Experior Assessments) at 1-800-532-2169. Go to their website at prometric.com for the bulletin and details.

Oklahoma

Candidates are not required to complete pre-licensing education to sit for the state exam, but completing an exam preparation course can significantly increase the opportunity to pass on the first attempt.

Your state does not require specific education before you take the Life, Life & Health, or Property & Casualty exam to obtain a producer's license. However, Dearborn realizes that these exams are difficult to pass unless you spend a significant amount of time learning about the principles, products and markets associated with today's dynamic insurance career. That's why we recommend enrolling with Dearborn in an exam prep course. Options in your state may include a classroom location or through Kaplan Financials self-study materials available in textbook, online or webcast formats. You learn the important basics you will need to succeed on the state exam and succeed in your career. Check the website for program availability, to order, and to enroll. Feel free to contact Kaplan Financial at 800-521-3395 for more information about Kaplan Financials programs.

To get a *Licensing Exam Candidate Handbook* or schedule an exam, call Promissor at 1-877-540-5830. Go to their website at promissor.com for the handbook and more details.

Oregon

Candidates must complete pre-licensing courses from an approved school to consist of eight (8) hours on Oregon laws and regulations, plus forty (40) hours for General Lines Insurance, thirty (30) hours for Life Insurance, twelve (12) hours for Health Insurance and twenty (20) hours for Personal Lines.

To get *Licensing Information Bulletin* or schedule an exam, call Promissor at 1-800-274-7003. Go to their website at promissor.com for the Bulletin and details.

Effective January 1, 2008, the pre-license education requirement for life will decrease from thirty (30) hours to twenty (20) hours, requirement for health will increase from twelve (12) hours to twenty (20) hours. An insurance degree from an accredited college or university will satisfy the pre-licensing requirement.

Pennsylvania

Candidates are required to complete twenty-four (24) hours of pre-licensing education (including 3 credit hours of ethics), through classroom or an approved correspondence self-study program. Self-study courses must be monitored by a disinterested third party that is not a relative or immediate supervisor of the candidate.

To get a Licensing Information Bulletin or schedule an exam, call Thomson Prometric (formerly Experior Assessments) at 1-800-715-2418. Go to their website at prometric.com for the bulletin and details.

Rhode Island

Candidates for a Life and/or Variable Life/Variable Annuities producer license must complete a thirty-two (32) hour education classroom course from an approved school. The course consists of twenty-six (26) hours of Life and Annuities, and six (6) hours of relevant state laws. For Accident & Health, candidates require twenty-six (26) hours of Accident & Health and six (6) hours of state law. For Accident & Health in addition to Life, a total of forty (40) hours are needed, consisting of thirty-two (32) hours of Life & Annuities and/or Accident & Health, and eight (8) hours of relevant state laws. For Property and/or Casualty, or Personal Lines Property & Casualty, candidates are required to have twenty-six (26) hours of Property & Casualty, and six (6) hours of relevant state laws. Credit and Limited licenses also require pre-licensing education.

To get a *Licensing Exam Candidate Handbook* or schedule an exam, call Promissor at 1-800-274-3739. Go to their website at promissor.com for a handbook and more details.

South Carolina

Candidates for producer licenses must complete a forty-hour pre-licensing education course in Life, Accident & Health and/or Property & Casualty, through classroom or an approved, supervised correspondence self-study program; or one year underwriting or marketing experience as an employee of a producer, insurer or their managers or general producer in all lines of insurance for the license(s) being applied for. Licensed insurance agents who have completed the forty-hour pre-licensing education coursework must pay the annual $10 fee to Thomson Prometric or they will not have their license renewed.

To obtain a *Licensing Examination Bulletin* or schedule an exam, call Thomson Prometric (formerly Experior Assessments) at 1-800-490-6548, or go to the website at prometric.com.

South Dakota

Candidates are not required to complete pre-licensing education to sit for the state exam, but completing an exam preparation course can significantly increase the opportunity to pass on the first attempt.

Your state does not require specific education before you take the Life, Life & Health, or Property & Casualty exam to obtain a producer's license. However, Dearborn realizes that these exams are difficult to pass unless you spend a significant amount of time learning about the principles, products and markets associated with today's dynamic insurance career. That's why we recommend enrolling with Dearborn in an exam prep course. Options in your state may include a classroom location or through our self-study materials available in textbook, online or webcast formats. You learn the important basics you will need to succeed on the state exam and succeed in your career. Check the website for program availability, to order, and to enroll. Feel free to contact Kaplan Financial at 800-521-3395 for more information about Kaplan Financials programs.

To get a *Licensing Information Bulletin* or schedule an exam, call Thomson Prometric (formerly Experior Assessments) at 1-800-864-8373. Go to their website at prometric.com for the bulletin and details.

Tennessee

Candidates must complete education for each line of insurance: Life (20 hours), Accident & Health (20 hours), Property (20 hours), Casualty (20 hours), Personal (30 hours) and Title (5 hours). Courses can be classroom, or a combined classroom/approved correspondence self-study program, with no more than 20 percent self-study.

To get a *Licensing Exam Candidate Handbook* or schedule an exam, call Promissor at 1-800-274-4957. Go to their website at promissor.com for a handbook and more details.

Texas

Applicants may receive a temporary ninety-day license before they pass the required examination if their sponsoring company, producer or agency requests it. Applications for temporary licensure should be sent to Promissor. The applicant must then complete forty (40) hours of training provided by the appointing insurance company or general lines producer/ agency within fourteen (14) days of the date of license application. Adjusters may qualify by passing an exam or by successfully completing a TDI-approved course.

To get an *Insurance Licensing Candidate Handbook* or schedule an exam, call Promissor at 1-888-204-6244. Go to their website at http://www.promissor.com for the handbook and details.

Utah

Candidates are not required to complete pre-licensing education to sit for the state exam, but completing an exam preparation course can significantly increase the opportunity to pass on the first attempt.

Your state does not require specific education before you take the Life, Life & Health, or Property & Casualty exam to obtain a producer's license. However, Dearborn realizes that these exams are difficult to pass unless you spend a significant amount of time learning about the principles, products and markets associated with today's dynamic insurance career. That's why we recommend enrolling with Dearborn in an exam prep course, which can be taken at one of Kaplan Financials convenient classroom locations or through Kaplan Financials self-study option available in text- book, online or webcast formats. You learn the important basics you will need to succeed on the state exam and succeed in your career. Feel free to contact Kaplan Financial at 800-521-3395 for more information about Kaplan Financials programs, to order, or to enroll.

To get a *Licensing Information Bulletin* or schedule an exam, call Thomson Prometric (formerly Experior Assessments) at 1-800-697-8947. Go to their website at prometric.com for the bulletin and details.

Vermont

Candidates are not required to complete pre-licensing education to sit for the state exam, but completing an exam preparation course can significantly increase the opportunity to pass on the first attempt.

Your state does not require specific education before you take the Life, Life & Health, or Property & Casualty exam to obtain a producer's license. However, Dearborn realizes that these exams are difficult to pass unless you spend a significant amount of time learning about the principles, products and markets associated with today's dynamic insurance career. That's why we recommend enrolling with Dearborn in an exam prep course. Options in your state may include a classroom location or through Kaplan Financials self-study materials available in textbook, online or webcast formats. You learn the important basics you will need to succeed on the state exam and succeed in your career. Check the website for program availability, to order, and to enroll. Feel free to contact Kaplan Financial at 800-521-3395 for more information about Kaplan Financials programs.

To get a *Licensing Information Bulletin* or schedule an exam, call Thomson Prometric (formerly Experior Assessments) at 1-800-868-6113. Go to their website at prometric.com for the bulletin and details.

Virginia

Candidates are not required to complete pre-licensing education to sit for the state exam, but completing an exam preparation course can significantly increase the opportunity to pass on the first attempt.

Your state does not require specific education before you take the Life, Life & Health, or Property & Casualty exam to obtain a producer's license. However, Dearborn realizes that these exams are difficult to pass unless you spend a significant amount of time learning about the principles, products and markets associated with today's dynamic insurance career. That's why we recommend enrolling with Dearborn in an exam prep course, which can be taken at one of Kaplan Financials convenient classroom locations or through Kaplan Financials self-study option available in text- book, online or webcast formats. You learn the important basics you will need to succeed on the state exam and succeed in your career. Feel free to contact Kaplan Financial at 800-521-3395 for more information about Kaplan Financials programs, to order, or to enroll.

To get a *Licensing Information Bulletin* or schedule an exam, call Thomson Prometric (formerly Experior Assessments) at 1-800-856-4308. Go to their website at prometric.com for the bulletin and details.

Washington

Candidates must complete both a four (4) hour classroom course on statutes and regulations, and a sixteen-hour classroom course for each line of insurance (Life, Disability, Property, or Casualty). A separate certificate is issued for the statutes and regulations course.

To get a *Licensing Exam Candidate Handbook* or schedule an exam, call Promissor at 1-800-274-8949. Go to their website at promissor.com for a handbook and more details.

West Virginia

Applicants must complete pre-licensing education courses as follows: Life-only (20 hours); Accident & Sickness (A&S) only (20 hours); Life and A&S (40 hours); Property & Casualty (40 hours); Personal Lines (20 hours). Courses may be taken through classroom or an approved correspondence self-study program.

To get a *Licensing Exam Candidate Handbook* or schedule an exam, call Promissor at 1-800-274-2614. Go to their website at promissor.com for a handbook and more details.

Wisconsin

Candidates must complete pre-licensing courses at an approved school. Education requirements are eight (8) hours of principles of insurance, WI insurance laws and ethics, plus twelve (12) hours specific to the license line (Life, Health, Property, Casualty, Personal lines). For example, a Life and Health licensee would need thirty-two (32) hours of pre-licensing education, eight (8) hours on principles, laws and ethics, plus twelve (12) hours Life plus twelve (12) hours Health.

To get a *Licensing Exam Candidate Handbook* or schedule an exam, call Promissor at 1-800-204-6216. Go to their website at promissor.com for a handbook and more details.

Wyoming

Candidates are not required to complete pre-licensing education to sit for the state exam, but completing an exam preparation course can significantly increase the opportunity to pass on the first attempt.

Your state does not require specific education before you take the Life, Life & Health, or Property & Casualty exam to obtain a producer's license. However, Dearborn realizes that these exams are difficult to pass unless you spend a significant amount of time learning about the principles, products and markets associated with today's dynamic insurance career. That's why we recommend enrolling with Dearborn in an exam prep course. Options in your state may include a classroom location or through Kaplan Financials self-study materials available in textbook, online or webcast formats. You learn the important basics you will need to succeed on the state exam and succeed in your career. Check the website for program availability, to order, and to enroll. Feel free to contact Kaplan Financial at 800-521-3395 for more information about Kaplan Financials programs.

To get a *Licensing Information Bulletin* or schedule an exam, call Thomson Prometric (formerly Experior Assessments) at 1-800-864-3946. Go to their website at prometric.com for the bulletin and details.

"Implementing the ideas in Jeff's book can help you create a solid business plan and, eventually, a successful and thriving agency."

—Dr. Robert P. Hartwig
President
Insurance Information Institute

Are you a sales manager and would like to teach the concepts presented in this book to your sales team?

Contact The Jeff Hastings Agency for workshops, books, and additional resources.

As a Sales Manager, you know there is more to running a successful business than simply selling insurance. Jeff Hastings has created a workshop which coincides with the systems presented to you in this book. This workshop will help you:

Get new agents off to a quick start

- Motivate veteran agents
- Create a vision for success
- Develop a solid foundation in which to build an agency
- Hire the right people and teach them the right things to do
- Develop their winning team
- Create systems for life insurance sales success

Contact us today!

Jeff Hastings Agency
11200 Westheimer #520
Houston, TX 77042
281-752-6565 JeffHastingsAgency.com

The EMyth Platform Everything you need to create the business you want

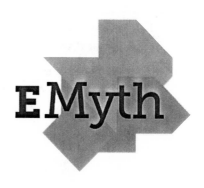

We wrote the book on systemization. We know how important it is to create a usable, scalable business. We also know the systems aren't the solution—they are the destination.

EMyth invented business coaching in 1978. Now, we've reimagined it—bringing the best of the legendary EMyth business development process forward for the modern business leader. At EMyth, we'll help you discover, or rediscover, your passion for what you do! If done right, your business should serve your life—not become it!

We created the world's first business coaching platform where you can learn to define your unique brand, systematize your operations, and delight your customers.

THE PLATFORM FEATURES:

- Self-paced lessons to develop every aspect of your business
- Each lesson begins with a video introducing the topic.
- The lessons are laid out in simple, clean text and are supported with examples, video, and helpful data.
- Our intuitive navigation lets you know exactly where you are in the lesson.
- The lessons are designed to challenge you.
- You'll tackle issues every business faces—from leadership to marketing and everything in between.

- You will create a library of key documents for your business and the steps to implement them immediately.
- Premium websites with access to premium webinars and access to archive covering topics such as leadership, self-organization, budgeting, sales, project management and branding.

FREE 30-DAY TRIAL

GET STARTED TODAY!

After the free trial ends, for only $100 per month and no monthly contract, you will receive everything mentioned above plus valuable insight from EMyth coaches so you can work more effectively on your business.

Contact Certified EMyth Business Coach Jeff Hastings at: jhastings@coach.emyth.com or to sign-up for the following services, go to:

- **Web Services Only: http://bit.ly/emythcoach**
- **Coaching Services: coach.emyth.com/jeffhastings**